FISHING FOR COMPLIMENTS

A Collection of Recipes from the

SHEDD AQUARIUM

C H I C A G O

This cookbook is a collection of favorite recipes, which are not necessarily original recipes.

Published by Shedd Aquarium Society
Copyright 1996 Shedd Aquarium Society
1200 South Lake Shore Drive
Chicago, Illinois 60605
312-939-2426

ISBN: 0-9611074-1-3

Edited and Manufactured by
Favorite Recipes® Press
P.O. Box 305142
Nashville, Tennessee 37230
1-800-358-0560

First Printing: 1996
10,000 copies
Book Design by Shedd Aquarium Planning and Design

Fishing for Compliments Committee

Winnie Clark, Chairman
Bonney Pope, Co-Chairman

Nancy Cody
Audrey Head
Anne Hokin
Anne Krebs
Sandi Muehlhauser
Stephanie Sick
Mary Smith
Gisela Zech

Special Thanks

Joan Freehling
Shedd Aquarium, Planning and Design
Jeff Woolford, Shedd Aquarium Executive Chef
The Marriott Corporation
Favorite Recipes® Press

Introduction

The oceans, lakes, streams, and rivers of the world are a continuing aquatic inspiration, but few people ever have the opportunity to see and appreciate all the fishes and marine mammals on our planet. Bringing these great creatures from around the world to the Midwest was the motivation for building the Shedd Aquarium in 1930.

The Aquarium's popularity since its opening reinforces John Graves Shedd's belief that this type of institution would play an important role in Chicago's cultural development. In 1931, more than four million visitors viewed the "wonders from far-off seas," as heralded by the newspapers of the day. More than 75 million people have passed through the bronze front doors to the Shedd Aquarium during the last six decades.

We have seen many changes since those early days. With 8,000 animals, representing more than 650 species, all under one roof, the Shedd Aquarium has one of the most comprehensive aquatic collections in the world. The Oceanarium, opened in 1991, is now home to whales, dolphins, sea otters, penguins, and harbor seals. Aquatic animals from every region of the world inhabit the 200 displays in the galleries of the original building. On any given day, you find yourself face to face with a host of engaging and exotic creatures.

Shedd Aquarium is grateful for all of the support it receives from its members, contributors, staff, and volunteers, as well as the millions of friends who visit each year. *Fishing for Compliments* is one example of ways these supporters become involved in ensuring the future of this wonderful institution. Throughout this book, you will find recipes from Shedd Aquarium members, Trustees, Governing Members, Auxiliary Society, volunteers, staff, and local business people.

"Shedd Aquarium promotes the enjoyment, appreciation, and effective conservation of aquatic life and its environments through education, research, and public display."

Table of Contents

APPETIZERS

Appetizers
Bleu Cheese and Bacon Rolls

1 pound bacon
1 (16-ounce) loaf white bread, sliced
1 (5-ounce) jar bleu cheese spread

Cut each slice of bacon into halves; set aside. Trim the crusts from the bread
and cut each slice into halves. Spread the bread with the bleu cheese spread. Roll up to
enclose filling. Wrap each with a bacon half and secure with a wooden pick. Place on a
baking sheet. Bake at 375 degrees for 10 minutes or until bacon is crispy.
Yield: 28 to 40 servings

Barb Stockton

Shedd Aquarium is the site of one of the most
breathtaking views of Chicago's skyline.

Cheese and Sausage Balls

1 (16-ounce) package hot sausage
1 (16-ounce) package sharp Cheddar cheese
2^1/$_2$ cups baking mix

Brown the sausage in a large skillet over medium heat, stirring until crumbly;
do not drain. Cube the cheese. Add to the sausage. Cook over low heat until the
cheese is melted, stirring constantly. Stir the baking mix 1 cup at a time into the
cheese and sausage mixture. Remove from heat and let stand until cool. Shape
the mixture into 1-inch balls. Place on a large baking sheet. Place in the
freezer for 20 minutes. Store in plastic bags until needed. Place on a baking sheet.
Bake at 375 degrees for 12 to 15 minutes or until browned and heated through.
Yield: 50 to 60 servings

Mrs. Thomas C. Clark

Cheese and Meat Pizzas

1 envelope dry yeast
1 teaspoon sugar
$2/3$ cup warm water
$1 1/2$ cups flour
$2/3$ cup cornmeal
$1/2$ teaspoon salt
$1/3$ cup plus 2 tablespoons olive oil
1 head garlic, separated, peeled
$1/2$ red onion, thinly sliced
1 ounce Parmesan cheese, grated
1 ounce asiago cheese, shredded
1 ounce provolone or mozzarella cheese, shredded
4 ounces prosciutto, thinly sliced
4 ounces cappicola, thinly sliced
1 cup coarsely chopped walnuts, toasted
$1/2$ cup chopped basil

Dissolve the yeast in a mixture of the sugar and warm water. Combine
the flour, cornmeal and salt in a large bowl. Stir in the yeast mixture and 2 tablespoons
of the olive oil. Knead the mixture until the dough is smooth and elastic. Place in a
greased bowl, turning to grease the surface. Let rise, covered, for 1 hour or until doubled
in bulk. Divide the dough into halves. Roll out into 8-inch circles on a floured surface.
Place on a baking sheet; set aside. Drizzle the remaining $1/3$ cup olive oil over the
garlic in a small baking dish. Bake at 350 degrees for 30 minutes. Mash the garlic
and spread over the prepared dough circles. Layer each circle with equal amounts of
onion, Parmesan cheese, asiago, provolone, prosciutto, cappicola, walnuts and
basil. Bake at 400 degrees for 15 minutes or until the cheese is browned and
bubbly. Slice each pizza into 8 to 10 slices to serve.
May substitute similar cheeses for those listed.
Yield: 16 to 20 servings

James A. Esposito

Crostini with Pesto

This quick recipe for this delicious appetizer was given to me by Becky Hostetter, co-owner of Essential Edibles, a vegetarian restaurant in Indianapolis.

1 garlic-parmesan, spinach or plain baguette
Olive oil
1 cup Basic Pesto Sauce (page 101)
1 cup grated Parmesan cheese

Cut the bread into ¼-inch slices. Brush each side of the bread with olive oil. Place on a broiler pan. Bake at 350 degrees for 3 minutes or until toasted; turn and toast the other side. Spread one side evenly with the pesto sauce; top with the Parmesan cheese. Broil 2 inches from the heat source for 5 minutes or until bubbly.
Yield: 15 to 18 servings

Beverly G. Hudnut

Appetizers
Ham Delights

1 cup melted butter
3 tablespoons prepared mustard
3 tablespoons poppy seeds
1 medium onion, finely chopped
1 teaspoon Worcestershire sauce
1 (40-count) package party rolls
1 pound boiled ham, shredded
1/3 pound Swiss cheese, thinly sliced

Combine the butter, mustard, poppy seeds, onion and Worcestershire
sauce in a small bowl; mix well. Slice the rolls into halves crosswise; remove the top
half. Spread each half with the mustard mixture. Layer the bottom half
with the ham and cheese. Replace the top half. Place on a baking sheet; wrap
with foil. Bake at 400 degrees for 10 minutes or until the cheese is melted.
Yield: 40 servings

Louise Kuca

Swiss Cheese Appetizers

8 ounces Swiss cheese, shredded
4 slices bacon, crisp-fried, crumbled
3/4 cup mayonnaise
1/2 cup chopped black olives
1/4 cup chopped onion
1 1/2 tablespoons chopped parsley
Caraway seeds to taste
1 loaf party rye bread

Combine the cheese, bacon, mayonnaise, olives, onion, parsley and
caraway seeds in a medium bowl; mix well. Spread over slices of the bread. Place
on a baking sheet. Bake at 400 degrees for 5 to 7 minutes or until the cheese is melted.
May prepare ahead and store in the refrigerator before baking.
Yield: 24 servings

Ann Rita Lee

Spinach Cheese Pitas

1 medium onion, finely chopped
1/4 cup olive oil
1 (10-ounce) package frozen spinach, thawed, drained
1/4 cup bread crumbs
8 ounces feta cheese, crumbled
6 ounces pot cheese
3 eggs, beaten
6 to 7 whole pitas
1/2 cup melted butter or margarine

Sauté the onion in the olive oil in a skillet for 5 minutes. Add the spinach. Simmer over low heat until the spinach begins to dry out, stirring occasionally. Remove from heat. Stir in the bread crumbs. Combine the feta cheese and pot cheese with the eggs in a medium bowl; beat well. Add to the spinach mixture, stirring well. Brush the pitas with the melted butter. Spread the spinach mixture evenly over the pitas. Place on a baking sheet. Bake at 425 degrees for 20 minutes. Cut into quarters and serve warm.

Yield: 24 to 28 servings

Linda Wilson

Spinach Squares

1/2 cup butter
3 eggs, beaten
1 cup flour
1 teaspoon salt
1 teaspoon baking powder
1 cup milk
16 ounces Monterey Jack cheese, shredded
1 (10-ounce) package frozen spinach, thawed, drained

Melt the butter in a 9x13-inch baking dish; set aside. Combine the eggs,
flour, salt, baking powder and milk in a medium bowl; beat well. Stir in the cheese
and spinach. Pour into the prepared pan. Bake at 350 degrees for 35 minutes.
Let stand for 30 minutes. Cut into 1-inch squares to serve.
Yields: 36 to 48 servings

Liz McCaffrey

Appetizers
Barbecued Shrimp

2 pounds extra-large shrimp, peeled, deveined
1 jar jalapeño pepper slices, drained
1 pound bacon, sliced
1 (18-ounce) jar barbecue sauce

Cut a slit into the back of each shrimp. Place a slice of the jalapeño pepper into the slit. Cut bacon slices into halves. Wrap each shrimp with a bacon half, securing with a wooden pick. Place the shrimp on the grill rack over hot coals. Grill for 5 to 10 minutes or until the shrimp are pink and the bacon is cooked through, basting frequently with the barbecue sauce.
Yield: 8 servings

Gerd H. Switzer

Herbed Shrimp with Basil Mayonnaise

3/4 cup olive oil
2 tablespoons lemon juice
1 tablespoon minced parsley
2 cloves of garlic, crushed
1 teaspoon salt
1/2 teaspoon oregano
Pepper to taste
2 pounds (about 56) shrimp
Basil Mayonnaise (page 21)

Combine the olive oil, lemon juice, parsley, garlic, salt, oregano and
pepper in a shallow dish; mix well. Rinse the shrimp and devein, but do not
remove the shells. Place the shrimp in the herb mixture. Marinate in the refrigerator for
2 hours, turning once. Let stand to reach room temperature. Place the shrimp
on skewers, discarding the marinade. Grill on a grill rack over hot coals for 3
minutes on each side or until cooked through. Remove from the skewers.
Arrange in a serving bowl. Garnish with lemon slices and parsley.
Serve with Basil Mayonnaise.
Yield: 6 to 8 servings

Basil Mayonnaise

2 egg yolks, at room temperature
2 teaspoons wine vinegar
1 teaspoon Dijon mustard
1/4 teaspoon salt
White pepper to taste
1 1/2 cups olive oil
2 cups basil leaves
1 clove of garlic, crushed
1/4 teaspoon salt
Black pepper to taste
Lemon juice to taste
Salt to taste

Combine the egg yolks, 1 teaspoon of the vinegar, mustard, 1/4 teaspoon
salt and white pepper in a blender container. Add 1/2 cup olive oil in a fine stream,
processing at high speed constantly. Add the remaining 1 teaspoon vinegar
and 1/2 cup of the olive oil, processing until thickened. Spoon into a medium bowl.
Combine the remaining 1/2 cup olive oil, basil, garlic, 1/4 teaspoon salt and
black pepper in a food processor fitted with a steel blade. Process until puréed.
Add to the mayonnaise mixture, whisking to blend.
Season with lemon juice and salt to taste.
Yield: 2 1/2 cups

Laris Gross

Cheese Dip in Bread

6 ounces cream cheese, softened
1 cup mayonnaise
1/4 cup sour cream
4 ounces Swiss cheese, shredded
4 ounces corned beef, chopped
1 1/2 green onions, chopped
1/2 teaspoon salt
1 round loaf sourdough bread

Beat the cream cheese, mayonnaise and sour cream in a mixer bowl
until light and fluffy. Stir in the Swiss cheese, corned beef, green onions and salt.
Scoop out the center from the loaf of bread, leaving a 1-inch wall; reserve the
bread. Cut the reserved bread into cubes and set aside. Spoon the cheese mixture
into the bread. Place on a baking sheet. Bake at 350 degrees for 1 hour.
Serve with the bread cubes or spread on crackers.
Yield: 6 to 10 servings

Mary Beth Baryl

Baked Party Bread

*When my husband was assigned to the U.S. Embassy in Panama, this became
a highly requested recipe in the international community and a definite hit for us.
It is now required fare at all family events.*

1 round loaf dark bread
1 bunch green onions, chopped
6 cloves of garlic, minced
2 tablespoons butter
8 ounces cream cheese, softened, cubed
2 cups sour cream
12 to 16 ounces Cheddar cheese, shredded
1 (14-ounce) can water-pack artichoke hearts, drained, cut into quarters

Cut a 5-inch-diameter circle from the top of the bread; reserve. Scoop
out the bread, leaving a 1-inch wall. Sauté the green onions and garlic in
the butter in a medium skillet until tender but not browned. Stir in the
cream cheese, sour cream and Cheddar cheese. Fold in the artichoke hearts.
Pour into the prepared bread shell. Cover with the reserved circle of bread.
Wrap in a double layer of heavy-duty foil; place on a baking sheet.
Bake at 350 degrees for 1 1/2 to 2 hours. Remove the foil.
Serve with garlic bread or crackers for dipping.
Yield: 20 servings

Cathleen E. Silveira

Appetizer Crab Meat Mold

2 (4-ounce) packages lemon gelatin
2$^1/_2$ cups boiling water
1 cup prepared chili sauce
$^1/_2$ cup pickle relish
$^1/_2$ cup chopped celery
2 (7-ounce) cans crab meat, drained, flaked

Dissolve the gelatin in the boiling water in a medium bowl.
Let cool slightly. Stir in the chili sauce, pickle relish and celery. Fold in the crab
meat. Pour into a nonstick 6-cup mold. Chill for 8 to 10 hours or
until firm. Unmold onto a watercress- or parsley-lined plate. Serve with
Russian or sour cream dressing and crackers. May substitute
1$^1/_2$ pounds fresh, peeled shrimp for the crab meat.
Yield: 6 to 8 servings

Muriel F. Fulton

Curried Dip

Curried Dip has been our standard hors d'oeuvre for twenty-five years.
It is easy, good and "addictive."

1 (9-ounce) jar Major Grey's original chutney
16 ounces cream cheese, softened
2 teaspoons curry powder
$1/2$ teaspoon dry mustard

Chop the chutney finely. Combine with the cream cheese, curry powder and
mustard in a medium bowl; mix well. Chill, covered, for 3 days to blend the flavors.
Stir well before serving. Serve with party rye bread or Triscuits. May
also spread on rye bread and broil for 1 minute.
Yield: 2 cups

Marcena W. Love

Chopped Eggplant Spread

*This recipe was handed down from my husband's
great-grandmother, Pauline Mendes.*

1 large eggplant
2 tablespoons water
$\frac{1}{2}$ large onion, sliced
$\frac{1}{2}$ large green bell pepper, sliced
$\frac{1}{2}$ cup (or more) canola oil
1 teaspoon salt
$\frac{1}{4}$ teaspoon pepper

Rinse the eggplant with cold water. Pierce 3 to 4 times with a fork. Place in a
microwave-safe baking dish with 2 tablespoons water; cover with plastic wrap.
Microwave on High for 6 minutes; turn over. Microwave for 6 minutes longer.
Let cool slightly. Chill for 1$\frac{1}{2}$ hours. Remove the stem and drain off
excess liquid. Cut into cubes. Process in a food processor with the onion and
green pepper until coarsely chopped. Add the oil gradually, processing until
of the desired consistency. Season with the salt and pepper. Serve with a variety
of crackers or levash bread. May prepare a day in advance.
Yield: 6 to 8 servings

Beverly M. Roitman

Appetizers
Potted Garlic

*A favorite recipe, we use this to go with dinner, or as a fun and different
hors d'oeuvre for a casual party. Rumor has it that if you roast the garlic in this
way, you won't get bad breath! (Or, perhaps, it's just that everyone eats it,
so that no one notices anyone else's breath!)*

3 large heads garlic (about 12 ounces)
1/2 teaspoon extra-virgin olive oil
Dash of salt
Freshly ground pepper to taste
1/2 teaspoon dried thyme, or 8 (1/2-inch) sprigs of fresh thyme

Cut off the top 1/4 of the garlic to expose the individual cloves.
Trim the side cloves to expose, but do not peel. Place root side down in an
earthenware garlic roaster or an ovenproof ramekin. Brush with the olive
oil; sprinkle with salt and pepper. Add the thyme to the roaster; cover tightly.
Bake at 400 degrees for 45 to 60 minutes or until the cloves are very soft. Cool
slightly. Spread over crusty Italian bread slices brushed with olive oil.
Yield: 15 servings

Vicky, Rick and Eric Stumpf

Gorgonzola Cheese Ball

Originally called "Insana's Delicious Cheese Ball," this recipe was given to me by my brother-in-law, Tino Insana. His mother made it for their family get-togethers. Tino's family has a long association with Chicago. He was at Second City in the 1970s and his dad, Silvio Insana, conducted the Chicago Symphony Orchestra, I believe in the 1940s. Tino's dad was conducting "Romeo and Juliette" the night Tino was born. Perhaps they celebrated later with a cheese ball.

8 ounces Gorgonzola cheese
8 ounces cream cheese, softened
2 teaspoons garlic salt or garlic powder
1/2 cup chopped nuts

Combine the Gorgonzola cheese, cream cheese and garlic salt in a
bowl; mix well. Shape into a ball. Roll in the chopped nuts to coat.
Wrap in plastic wrap; place in a covered container.
Chill until firm. Serve with crackers.
Yield: 15 servings

Jana Serrano

Appetizers
Hummus Bi Tahini

A quick, easy recipe. A Lebanese friend of mine in Paris said this was the best Hummus he has had, second to his mother's.

4 cups cooked chick-peas
1/2 cup prepared tahini (sesame seed paste)
1/3 cup warm water
1/3 cup olive oil
Juice of 3 to 4 lemons
5 cloves of garlic
1 1/2 teaspoons salt
2 teaspoons ground cumin
Freshly ground pepper to taste

Combine the chick-peas, tahini, water, olive oil and lemon juice
in a food processor container fitted with a steel blade. Process until smooth.
Add the garlic, salt, cumin and pepper, stirring well. Adjust seasonings. Pour
into a serving container. Chill, covered, until serving time. Garnish with
chopped tomatoes and cucumbers. Serve with pita bread wedges.
Yield: 4 cups

Shelly Szychowski and Mark Botelho

Tapenade

8 ounces kalamata olives, pitted
3 tablespoons capers
4 anchovy fillets
1 clove of garlic
Dash of cayenne pepper
1 teaspoon savory leaves
1/4 cup olive oil

Combine the olives, capers, anchovies, garlic, pepper, savory
and olive oil in a food processor container. Process until puréed.
May add lemon juice to obtain desired consistency.
Serve with fresh bread or crackers.
Yield: 3/4 cup

Betsy Schroeder

Appetizers
Vegetable Dip

*A simple recipe passed many years ago from my
mother (a wonderful cook) to me (a hopeless cook)!*

1 cup mayonnaise
1 teaspoon tarragon vinegar
$1/4$ teaspoon salt
Dash of pepper
$1/8$ teaspoon thyme
$1/4$ teaspoon curry powder
$1/2$ small onion, grated
2 tablespoons chili sauce

Combine the mayonnaise, vinegar, salt, pepper, thyme, curry powder,
onion and chili sauce in a bowl; mix well. Chill for several hours before serving.
Serve with fresh cauliflower, cucumbers, carrots and celery.
May substitute plain nonfat yogurt for the mayonnaise.
Yield: 8 servings

Peg Higgins

Festive Mexican Dip

16 ounces small curd cottage cheese, drained
8 ounces cream cheese, softened
1 envelope taco seasoning mix
2 bunches green onions, chopped
2 tomatoes, seeded, chopped
1 medium green bell pepper, chopped
2 cups shredded Cheddar cheese
1 (6-ounce) can sliced black olives, drained

Beat cottage cheese and cream cheese in a mixer bowl until
light and fluffy. Spread evenly over a serving platter. Sprinkle with half of the
taco seasoning mix. Layer with the green onions, tomatoes, green peppers, remaining
taco seasoning mix, Cheddar cheese and olives. Serve with tortilla chips.

Yield: 15 servings

Maureen Clennon

Peeb's Five-Layer Taco Dip

I've been preparing and bringing this dip to parties for the last eight years and it is always a big hit.

1 (16-ounce) can refried beans
2/3 cup prepared taco sauce
3/4 cup sour cream
1 cup seeded chopped tomatoes
1 (6-ounce) can chopped black olives, drained
1/2 cup shredded cheese for tacos

Combine the beans and 2 tablespoons of the taco sauce in a small bowl; mix well. Stir the remaining taco sauce into the sour cream in a bowl. Layer the bean mixture, sour cream mixture, tomatoes, olives and cheese in a 9-inch serving plate. Chill, covered, before serving. Serve with tortilla or corn chips.

Yield: 4 1/2 cups

P. B. Kral

Tuna à la Mexicana

A favorite of Mexican households before dinner or as a snack.

2 (6-ounce) cans tuna, drained
4 green onion tops, chopped
Juice of 1/2 lemon
1 (15-ounce) can chick-peas
2 tablespoons chopped cilantro
1 medium jalapeño, finely chopped (optional)
1 cup milk
2/3 tablespoon bread crumbs
2 tablespoons butter or margarine
Salt and pepper to taste
4 eggs, beaten

Flake the tuna into a medium bowl. Stir in the green onion tops and lemon juice. Drain the chick-peas, discarding the skins. Add to tuna mixture with cilantro and jalapeño, mixing with a fork. Combine the milk, bread crumbs, butter, salt and pepper in a saucepan. Cook over low heat until the mixture thickens, stirring occasionally. Stir into the tuna mixture. Add the eggs, mixing well. Spoon into a greased 8x10-inch baking dish. Bake at 400 degrees for 40 minutes or until browned and cooked through. Cool for 5 to 10 minutes. Cut into squares.

Serve with crackers or corn chips.

Yield: 12 servings

Estelle Gonzales-Walgreen

Broccoli Salad

3 large bunches broccoli
1 medium onion, chopped
8 ounces bacon, crisp-fried, crumbled
1 cup shredded Cheddar cheese
$1/2$ cup mayonnaise
$1/4$ cup sugar
1 tablespoon vinegar

Cut the broccoli heads into bite-size florets. Reserve the stalks for another purpose. Combine the broccoli florets, onion, bacon and cheese in a large bowl. Blend the mayonnaise, sugar and vinegar in a medium bowl. Pour the dressing over the salad and mix well. Serve chilled. May reduce the amount of bacon and cheese by $1/2$ and substitute low-fat or nonfat salad dressing for the mayonnaise dressing. May substitute 6 envelopes artificial sweetener for the sugar. May substitute a poppyseed dressing for the mayonnaise dressing.

Yield: 4 servings

Margaret Shurilla

The Pacific Northwest coastline is re-created in the Oceanarium.

Chinese Salad

Every time I have served this salad, people have just raved about it!

1 cup sugar
1/2 cup vinegar
1 cup vegetable oil
2 tablespoons soy sauce
2 packages ramen noodles
1 package sliced almonds
1 small jar sesame seeds
1/2 cup margarine
1 bunch bok choy, chopped, chilled
1 bunch green onions, chopped, chilled

Combine the sugar, vinegar, oil and soy sauce in a bowl and
mix well. Chill until needed. Break up the noodles in the unopened packages.
Discard the seasoning packets or reserve for another use. Sauté the noodles,
almonds and sesame seeds in the margarine in a skillet; set aside. Combine
the bok choy and green onions in a large bowl. Add the dressing
and mix well. Stir in the noodle mixture just before serving.
Yield: 6 servings

Helen B. Shimon

Finnish Salad

My daughter had this salad in Helsinki in 1988 when she was a student ambassador to Russia and Northern Europe. The salad, low on lettuce, was served without dressing, but we prefer a light dressing. It is a very attractive salad for a buffet. It can also be made in any size and served in individual bowls.

1 pound lettuce, shredded
3 (8-ounce) cans baby corn
2 (2-ounce) cans sliced black olives
1 pound fresh mushrooms, sliced
8 plum tomatoes, cut into halves, sliced
1 (8- to 10-ounce) bottle white wine vinaigrette salad dressing or
lemon pepper salad dressing

Place the lettuce in a large salad bowl. Layer the corn, olives, mushrooms and tomatoes over the lettuce. Pour the dressing over the salad.

Yield: 25 to 30 servings

Laris Gross

Mandarin Salad

This is especially nice in winter when tomatoes and other summer salad ingredients are not as readily available.

½ cup sugar
1 teaspoon dry mustard
1 teaspoon salt
1 tablespoon grated onion
⅓ cup cider vinegar
1 cup vegetable oil
1 tablespoon (or less) poppyseeds
½ cup sliced almonds
2 tablespoons sugar
Mixed lettuce and spinach, torn into bite-size pieces
2 to 4 green onions, thinly sliced
1 cup chopped celery
1 (11-ounce) can mandarin oranges, drained

Combine ½ cup sugar, dry mustard, salt, onion, vinegar, oil and poppyseeds in a covered glass jar and shake well. Let stand for several hours to allow the flavors to blend. Combine the almonds and 2 tablespoons sugar in a small heavy pan. Cook over very low heat until the sugar is dissolved and the almonds are glazed, stirring frequently. Spread on waxed paper to cool. Toss the lettuce, spinach, green onions and celery in a large bowl. Top with the mandarin oranges and almonds. Pour the dressing over the salad and toss to mix.
Yield: 6 to 8 servings

Carol Thomas

Orange and Jicama Salad with Cilantro Dressing

3 tablespoons balsamic vinegar
2 tablespoons orange juice
1/2 cup chopped cilantro
2 teaspoons Dijon mustard
1 clove of garlic, minced
1/2 teaspoon dried oregano
2/3 cup olive oil
Salt and pepper to taste
6 cups mixed red leaf radicchio and endive
3 oranges, peeled, sliced into rounds
1/2 small jicama, peeled, julienned
2 tablespoons toasted pine nuts
1/4 cup pomegranate seeds

Combine the vinegar, orange juice, cilantro, Dijon mustard, garlic and
oregano in a bowl and whisk to mix. Add the oil in a slow stream and whisk well.
Season with salt and pepper. Arrange the radicchio and endive on
individual plates. Arrange the oranges and jicama over the greens. Top with the
pine nuts and pomegranate seeds. Pour the dressing over the salad.
Yield: 6 to 8 servings

Mrs. John C. Pope

Spinach Salad

3/4 cup chopped Cheddar cheese
1/2 cup chopped celery
1/2 cup chopped onion
3 hard-cooked eggs, peeled, chopped
1 1/2 cups low-fat mayonnaise
1/4 cup horseradish
1 1/2 teaspoons vinegar
1/2 teaspoon salt
4 cups chopped spinach

Combine the cheese, celery, onion, eggs, mayonnaise,
horseradish, vinegar and salt in a medium bowl and mix well. Combine
with the spinach in a large bowl and toss well.
Yield: 8 servings

Mary J. Bauhs

Low-Calorie Potato Salad

6 large red potatoes, chopped
4 ribs celery, chopped
8 green onions, chopped
1/4 cup chopped green bell pepper
1/4 cup chopped red bell pepper
1/4 cup chopped fresh Italian parsley
1/4 cup capers, drained
1 teaspoon dillweed
1 teaspoon celery seeds
1/2 teaspoon salt
1/2 teaspoon freshly ground pepper
4 hard-cooked egg whites, chopped
1 cup plain nonfat yogurt
1/2 cup low-fat mayonnaise
2 tablespoons lemon juice
2 tablespoons apple cider vinegar
2 tablespoons Dijon mustard
1 teaspoon yellow mustard
1 tablespoon chopped fresh basil

Cook the potatoes in water to cover in a saucepan until tender;
drain well. Cool to room temperature. Combine the potatoes, celery,
green onions, bell peppers, parsley, capers, dillweed, celery seeds,
salt, pepper and egg whites in a large bowl and mix well. Combine the
yogurt, mayonnaise, lemon juice, vinegar, Dijon mustard, yellow mustard
and basil in a medium bowl and whisk to mix. Fold into the potato mixture.
Chill for several hours. Garnish with tomato wedges and basil strips.
Yield: 8 servings

Mrs. Peter B. Foreman

Wild Rice Salad

*Other than cooking the rice, which can be done ahead of time, this salad
can be put together in twenty minutes. It's great for potluck events, but be forewarned:
Carry copies of the recipe because you'll be besieged with requests for them.*

1 cup raisins
1 cup wild rice
4¼ cups water
1 cup pecan halves, or ¾ cup pecan pieces
¾ cup thinly sliced green onions
⅓ cup olive oil
¼ cup rice wine vinegar
¼ teaspoon freshly ground pepper, or to taste

Soak the raisins in hot water to cover until plump; drain well. Rinse the rice
several times. Cook the rice in 4¼ cups water in a rice steamer until the grains split open.
Spread the pecans in a single layer in a shallow baking pan. Bake at
350 degrees for 10 minutes or until toasted. Check the pecans as soon as
their aroma is noticeable. Mix the rice, raisins and green onions in a large bowl.
Whisk the olive oil, vinegar and pepper in a small bowl. Pour over the rice
mixture and toss. Chill, covered, until serving time. Add the pecans and mix lightly.
May increase the olive oil to ½ cup and the vinegar to ⅓ cup
if a larger amount of dressing is needed.
Yield: 12 servings

Karen Furnweger

Chinese Coleslaw

1 cup slivered almonds
4 packages ramen noodles
2 to 3 tablespoons margarine
1 medium head napa cabbage, chopped
1 bunch green onions, chopped
1 package prepared coleslaw
3 tablespoons soy sauce
1/4 cup cider vinegar
3/4 cup sugar
3/4 cup vegetable oil

Spread the almonds in a single layer in a shallow microwave-safe dish.
Microwave on High for 2 to 3 minutes or until toasted. Discard the seasoning packets
from the noodles or reserve for another use. Crumble the noodles. Sauté the noodles in the
margarine in a skillet until lightly browned. Combine the noodles, almonds, cabbage and
green onions in a large bowl and mix well. Add the slaw and mix well. Combine the soy
sauce, vinegar, sugar and oil in a covered jar or medium bowl; shake or mix well.
Pour over the salad. Chill for 30 to 60 minutes before serving.
Yield: 12 to 16 servings

Gina Maling

Soups and Salads
Sandi's Slaw

1 pound coleslaw
4 green onions, chopped
$^1/_2$ package raisins
2 packages slivered toasted almonds
1 (4-ounce) package sunflower seeds
2 packages chicken ramen noodles, crushed
$^1/_2$ cup vinegar
$^1/_2$ cup vegetable oil
$^1/_2$ cup sugar

Combine the coleslaw and green onions in a large bowl and mix well.
Mix the raisins, almonds, sunflower seeds and noodles together. Mix the vinegar, oil,
sugar and contents of the noodle seasoning packets in a small bowl. Add the raisin
mixture and vinegar mixture to the coleslaw mixture and toss well.
Yield: 6 to 8 servings

Mrs. G. Robert Muehlhauser

Soups and Salads
Antipasto Salad

3/4 cup safflower oil or olive oil
1/4 cup white wine vinegar
1/2 teaspoon garlic powder
2 tablespoons chopped fresh basil, or 1 teaspoon dried
1 teaspoon sugar
1 teaspoon salt
1/2 teaspoon pepper
3 1/2 ounces plain tortellini
3 1/2 ounces spinach tortellini
4 ounces macaroni twists
2 cups broccoli florets
1 (14-ounce) can artichoke hearts, drained, cut into quarters
1 (2-ounce) jar sliced pimento, drained
1 cup pitted black olives
6 slices Genoa salami
6 slices prosciutto, julienned
Chopped parsley to taste
Chopped scallions to taste
6 slices provolone cheese, shredded

Combine the oil, vinegar, garlic powder, basil, sugar, salt and pepper
in a blender container. Process until mixed. Cook the tortellini and macaroni using the
package directions; drain and rinse with cold water. Toss with half the dressing
in a bowl. Steam the broccoli in a saucepan or steamer for 3 to 5 minutes or until tender-
crisp. Combine with the artichoke hearts, pimento, olives, salami and prosciutto in a bowl
and mix well. Toss with the remaining dressing. Toss the pasta mixture with the vegetable
mixture. Chill for several hours. Stir in the parsley, scallions and cheese. Remove to a
decorative glass bowl. Serve over lettuce leaves. Serve with crusty French bread.
Yield: 8 to 10 servings

Gerd H. Switzer

Fresh Pasta Salad

1 package rotini pasta
1 medium bunch broccoli, cut into bite-size pieces
4 medium carrots, cut into bite-size pieces
3 plum tomatoes, cut into small pieces
1 small can sliced black olives, drained
2 jars marinated artichoke hearts, drained
1 bottle Italian salad dressing
Grated Parmesan cheese to taste (optional)

Cook the pasta using the package directions; drain and rinse.
Combine the pasta, broccoli, carrots, tomatoes, olives and artichoke hearts
in a bowl and toss well. Stir in the salad dressing. Top with the cheese. Chill
overnight. May add toasted pine nuts, sun-dried tomatoes or hearts of palm.
Yield: 4 to 8 servings

Linsey A. Foster

Kim's Pasta Salad

1 pound tri-color pasta
1 red onion, chopped
2 large red tomatoes, chopped
1 can hearts of palm, chopped
$1/2$ can black olives, cut into halves
2 cups chopped broccoli
$1/4$ cup olive oil
$1/2$ cup red wine vinegar
$1/4$ cup Dijon mustard

Cook the pasta using the package directions. Rinse in a colander under cool water for 3 minutes. Remove the pasta to a bowl and refrigerate until needed. Mix the onion, tomatoes, hearts of palm, olives and broccoli in a large bowl. Mix the olive oil, vinegar and Dijon mustard in a small bowl. Add additional mustard if the dressing tastes too weak or additional water if it tastes too strong. Combine the pasta, vegetable mixture and dressing in a bowl and toss well.

Yield: 10 servings

Kimberly C. Hamill

Mediterranean Pasta Salad

2/3 cup olive oil
3 tablespoons red wine vinegar
1/4 cup basil
2 tablespoons chopped green onions
2 tablespoons grated Parmesan cheese
1 1/4 teaspoons salt
1/4 teaspoon ground pepper
1 medium red bell pepper
1 medium green bell pepper
1 medium yellow bell pepper
12 ounces rotelle pasta, cooked, drained
8 ounces cherry tomatoes, sliced
1 can black olives, sliced
8 ounces mozzarella cheese, chopped

Combine the olive oil, vinegar, basil, green onions, Parmesan cheese, salt and
pepper in a blender container or food processor container. Process until smooth.
Cut the bell peppers into halves lengthwise; cut the halves crosswise into thin strips.
Combine the pasta, bell peppers, tomatoes, olives and mozzarella cheese in a
large bowl. Pour the dressing over the salad and toss well. Chill until serving time.
May serve cold or at room temperature.
Yield: 4 servings

Cindy and Garry Melnick

Riverbank Pasta Salad

2 packages cheese tortellini
1 green bell pepper, chopped
2 tomatoes, chopped
$1/2$ bunch broccoli, chopped
$1/4$ head cauliflower, chopped
1 small can sliced olives
1 can artichoke hearts
8 ounces mushrooms, sliced
$1/2$ package alfalfa sprouts
1 large bottle Italian salad dressing
Salt and pepper to taste
Olive oil (optional)

Cook the pasta using the package directions; drain and let cool.
Combine the pasta, green pepper, tomatoes, broccoli, cauliflower, olives,
artichoke hearts, mushrooms and alfalfa sprouts in a large bowl. Pour the dressing
over the salad and toss. Season with salt, pepper and a small amount
of olive oil. Chill overnight. Serve at room temperature. May add julienne strips
of leftover lunch meat at serving time. May substitute carrots, pea pods or
other vegetables for any of the listed vegetables.
Yield: 16 to 20 servings

Linda Wilson

Seafood Pasta Salad

1 cup multicolored pasta
1 cup crumbled or chopped feta cheese
8 crab sticks, chopped
2 scallions, trimmed, thinly sliced
1/2 green bell pepper, chopped
1/3 cup black olives
1/2 cup olive oil
1/4 cup red wine vinegar
1 tablespoon tomato paste
1 teaspoon sugar
1/8 teaspoon dry mustard, or to taste
1/2 teaspoon lemon juice
2 to 3 drops of anchovy extract, or to taste
1 tablespoon chopped fresh parsley

Cook the pasta just until tender using the package directions. Rinse with cold
water and drain. Combine the pasta, cheese, crab, scallions, green pepper and olives
in a large bowl. Combine the olive oil, vinegar, tomato paste, sugar, dry
mustard, lemon juice, anchovy extract and parsley in a medium bowl and mix well.
Pour over the salad and toss well. Chill until serving time.
Yield: 2 to 3 servings

Barbara Kramer Dibble

Tuna and Pepper Macaroni Salad

3 ounces elbow macaroni
1/4 cup chopped green bell pepper
1/4 cup chopped red bell pepper
1/4 cup chopped orange bell pepper
1/4 cup chopped yellow bell pepper
1 (6-ounce) can water-pack tuna, drained
1 tablespoon ranch salad dressing
1 tablespoon lemon juice
Salt and pepper to taste
Leaf lettuce

Cook the macaroni al dente using the package directions; rinse with cold water and drain well. Combine the pasta, bell peppers, tuna, salad dressing, lemon juice, salt and pepper in a large bowl and mix well. Chill until serving time. Serve over lettuce. Increase the lemon juice to 1 1/2 tablespoons if doubling this recipe.

Yield: 2 servings

Charis Lehnert

Mrs. Daddario's Bleu Cheese Dressing

1 quart mayonnaise
1 1/2 cups buttermilk
1 teaspoon garlic powder
1 teaspoon salt
2 tablespoons chopped parsley or parsley flakes
6 ounces bleu cheese or Roquefort cheese, at room temperature

Combine the mayonnaise, buttermilk, garlic powder, salt and
parsley in a bowl and mix well. Break the cheese into pieces into the
mayonnaise mixture; mix well. Chill thoroughly.
Yield: 1 1/2 quarts

David L. Epstein

Pilot's House Dressing

4 cups olive oil
$^1/_2$ cup Italian seasoning
$^1/_2$ cup Worcestershire sauce
1 cup balsamic vinegar
$^1/_4$ cup honey
2 cups Parmesan cheese
$^1/_4$ cup bleu cheese
$^1/_4$ cup feta cheese
1 tablespoon white pepper
3 cloves of fresh garlic, minced

Combine all ingredients in the order listed in a blender container or
food processor, processing constantly until mixed. Blend for 5 minutes longer.
This dressing must be stirred before each serving.
Yield: $4^1/_2$ cups

Nan Graves

Salad Dressing

1 cup sugar
1 cup vegetable oil
$^1/_4$ cup catsup
1 teaspoon Worcestershire sauce
1 teaspoon salt
$^1/_4$ teaspoon cloves
1 small onion, chopped
$^1/_3$ cup vinegar

Combine the sugar, oil, catsup, Worcestershire sauce, salt, cloves, onion and vinegar in a large bowl and mix well. The mixture will be thick.

Yield: 1 pint

Joan B. Hamill

Mom's Vinaigrette Salad Dressing

Mother's salad dressing gets rave reviews, but we could never convince her to challenge Paul Newman's commercial venture. However, she gladly taught her kids the basic recipe and encouraged improvisation and experimentation. This is the basic recipe. We often add some grated lemon peel, fresh basil, even a clove of garlic to flavor the dressing slightly.

1 teaspoon Crazy Jane's mixed-up salt
1/4 to 1/2 teaspoon freshly ground black pepper
1/4 to 1/2 teaspoon lemon pepper
1 teaspoon dried salad herbs
1/2 teaspoon dried tarragon
2 teaspoons Dijon mustard
1 teaspoon lemon juice
1/4 teaspoon Worcestershire sauce
1/3 cup white wine tarragon vinegar
1/2 cup olive oil
1/2 cup vegetable oil

Combine the first 9 ingredients in a glass or plastic container,
stirring until the salt is dissolved. Add the olive oil and vegetable
oil and mix well. Store in the refrigerator.
Yield: 1 1/3 cups

Peter Shedd Reed

Black Bean Soup

We used less spice and too much oregano at first; this is our revised version. I suggest you fine-tune to your own taste.

2 cups chopped onions
4 teaspoons vegetable oil
1 teaspoon minced garlic
1 teaspoon cumin
1/4 teaspoon cayenne
1 1/2 teaspoons ground coriander
1 teaspoon oregano
1/2 teaspoon thyme
4 cups chicken broth
2 cans black beans
1/2 cup dry sherry (optional)

Cook the onions in the oil in a large saucepan for 5 minutes. Add the garlic, cumin, cayenne, coriander, oregano and thyme. Cook for 1 minute. Add the chicken broth and beans. Bring to a boil; reduce the heat. Simmer for 10 minutes. Purée the soup in small batches in a blender. Reheat if needed. Stir in the sherry.
Yield: 4 servings

Hal Matthies

Ham and Bean Chili

1 1/4 pounds dried lima beans
12 ounces chopped cooked ham
1 (8-ounce) can whole-kernel corn, drained
3/4 cup chopped onion
4 teaspoons chili powder
4 teaspoons Worcestershire sauce
1 (10-ounce) can tomato soup
2 teaspoons salt
1 teaspoon Tabasco sauce
1 1/4 cups water

Rinse and sort the beans. Combine the beans with water to cover in a large
soup pot. Cover and bring to a boil; reduce the heat. Simmer for 1 hour. Add the
ham, corn, onion, chili powder, Worcestershire sauce, tomato soup, salt, Tabasco
sauce and water. Simmer for 1 hour, stirring frequently and
adding additional water if needed.
Yield: 6 servings

Sandra K. Crown

Hal's Consensus Chili

*This was culled from a dozen chili recipes. Add some red pepper flakes
($^1/_2$ teaspoon to start) and go up to four-alarm chili.*

1 pound ground beef
1 onion, chopped
1 tablespoon garlic
1 green bell pepper, chopped
Vegetable oil
$^1/_2$ teaspoon cumin
1 tablespoon paprika
2 tablespoons chili powder
1 can beef broth
1 (14-ounce) can Mexican tomatoes
1 (8-ounce) can tomato sauce
1 (15-ounce) can kidney beans

Brown the ground beef in a skillet, stirring until crumbly; drain well. Sauté the
onion, garlic and green pepper in a small amount of oil in a skillet. Combine
the onion mixture, ground beef, cumin, paprika, chili powder, beef broth, tomatoes,
tomato sauce and beans in a large pot. Simmer for 1 hour.

Yield: 4 servings

Hal Matthies

Peter Barrett Latin Alumni Special Chili

4 cups kidney beans
5 tablespoons shortening
1 cup coarsely chopped onion
4 cloves of garlic, finely chopped
1/2 cup chopped green bell pepper
2 pounds coarsely ground lean beef
4 cups peeled fresh tomatoes, cut into quarters
1 teaspoon salt
1/4 cup chili powder
2 tablespoons cumin
1 tablespoon wine vinegar
1 tablespoon brown sugar
1 to 2 tablespoons chopped bottled hot or
extra-hot jalapeños or hot or extra-hot chilipiquin sauce

Sort and rinse the beans. Soak the beans in water to cover overnight;
drain well. Melt the shortening in a Dutch oven or large cast-iron skillet. Sauté the onion,
garlic and green pepper in the shortening until the onion is translucent. Add
the ground beef. Cook until the ground beef is browned, stirring until the ground beef is
crumbly. Plunge the tomatoes into boiling water for 1 minute; drain. Remove the peel
and cut into quarters. Add to the ground beef mixture with the beans, salt, chili powder,
cumin, vinegar, brown sugar and jalapeños. Simmer, covered, for 1 1/2 to 2 hours,
adding water if needed. Let cool. Store in the refrigerator for 1 to 2 days before reheating.
Garnish with chopped onion, sour cream and hot seasoning. Serve with oyster crackers
and cold beer. May substitute pinto beans for kidney beans.
Yield: 9 to 14 servings

Peter Barrett

Harpy Soup Plus

*Make this wonderful warm-weather soup during the hot summer days
and refrigerate it for serving in the next few days. It gets better and better.
It's a favorite of a fun group of old friends!*

1 jar clamato juice
2 tablespoons white wine vinegar
2 tablespoons vegetable oil
1 tablespoon sugar
1 teaspoon dill
1/2 cup sliced cucumber
Tabasco sauce to taste
1 avocado, finely chopped
3 ounces cream cheese, cubed
1 can small shrimp
1/3 cup sliced scallions
1 small tomato, chopped

Combine the clamato juice, vinegar, oil, sugar, dill, cucumber, Tabasco
sauce, avocado, cream cheese, shrimp, scallions and tomato in a large bowl and
mix well. Chill until serving time. Ladle into soup bowls. Garnish each serving
with a dollop of sour cream sprinkled with fresh dill.
Yield: 4 servings

Penny Beattie

Mushroom Barley Soup

8 ounces mushrooms, sliced
1 medium onion, chopped
1/3 cup butter
1/3 cup flour
2 cups water
3 cups milk
1/2 cup quick-cooking barley
2 teaspoons Worcestershire sauce
1 teaspoon salt (optional)
1 teaspoon parsley flakes
1/2 teaspoon white or black pepper

Sauté the mushrooms and onion in the butter in a saucepan. Blend in
the flour, stirring constantly. Add a mixture of the water and milk. Stir in the barley,
Worcestershire sauce, salt, parsley flakes and pepper. Bring to a boil, stirring occasionally;
reduce the heat. Simmer, covered, for 10 to 12 minutes or until the barley is tender.
May add additional milk if the soup becomes too thick upon standing.
Yield: 8 to 10 servings

Arthur F. Jeczala

Roasted Red Pepper Soup

4 large red bell peppers, or 1 (24-ounce) jar roasted red peppers
1 (28-ounce) can tomatoes
1 tablespoon olive oil
3 large shallots, minced
1 clove of garlic, minced
1 cup dry red wine
1 teaspoon sugar
1 teaspoon salt
1/2 teaspoon pepper
1 cup tomato juice
1 teaspoon minced sage

Purée 3 of the red peppers in a blender or food processor. Cut the remaining
red pepper into thin strips. Purée the tomatoes in a blender or food processor.
Heat the olive oil in a large saucepan. Add the shallots and garlic.
Cook for 3 minutes or until softened. Add the tomatoes, wine, sugar, salt, pepper and
puréed red peppers and mix well. Bring to a boil. Simmer for 20 minutes.
Stir in the tomato juice and sage. Serve hot or cold, ladled into soup
bowls and garnished with the red pepper strips.
Yield: 8 to 10 servings

Mrs. John C. Pope

Tortellini Soup with Tomatoes

2 (8-ounce) packages fresh cheese tortellini
6 cups canned or homemade chicken broth
2 green onions, chopped
1 (14-ounce) can chopped Italian tomatoes
Freshly grated Parmesan cheese to taste
Freshly ground pepper to taste

Cook the tortellini using the package directions; drain and rinse lightly
with cold water. Bring the chicken broth to a light simmer in a large pot. Add the green
onions, undrained tomatoes and pasta. Cook for 3 to 4 minutes or until heated
through. Top with the cheese. Sprinkle with the pepper. Serve immediately.
Serve with a green salad and lots of hard, crusty Italian bread.
Yield: 4 to 6 servings

Cynthia C. Flannery, Jr.

Soups and Salads
Crab Cream Soup

1 large cucumber, peeled, finely chopped
1/2 cup whipping cream
2 teaspoons Worcestershire sauce
1 tablespoon Dijon mustard
2 (10-ounce) cans cream of mushroom soup
Salt and pepper to taste
1 pound cooked crab meat
2 tablespoons sherry
2 teaspoons minced dillweed or sprigs of dill

Combine the cucumber, whipping cream, Worcestershire sauce, Dijon mustard
and soup in a blender container. Process until smooth. Season with salt
and pepper. Chill for 6 hours. Add the crab meat and sherry. Cook in a saucepan
until heated through. Ladle into soup bowls. Top with the dill. May serve cold.
Yield: 8 servings

Laris Gross

Crab Gumbo

1 (10-ounce) can cream of tomato soup
1 (10-ounce) can split pea soup
2 soup cans milk
1 can consommé
2 cans crab meat
1 to 2 tablespoons sherry, or to taste

Combine the tomato soup, split pea soup, milk and consommé in a saucepan. Bring to a simmer. Add the crab meat. Simmer for 5 minutes. Stir in the sherry. Ladle into bowls. Garnish with croutons.
Yield: 5 to 6 servings

Charles C. Haffner II

Keys Conch Chowder

This recipe was given to William Braker, former director of the Shedd Aquarium, by Wilma Hansen, wife of Captain Emil Hansen, who was captain of the Miami Seaquarium's collecting boat and who later became captain of the Coral Reef, Shedd Aquarium's first large collecting boat. It is a favorite of collecting crews aboard the Coral Reef.

1 pound conch, cleaned, coarsely ground
4 slices bacon, chopped
2 large onions, chopped
3 cloves of garlic, crushed
1 green bell pepper, chopped
1 (6-ounce) can tomato paste
1 (8-ounce) can tomato sauce
3 medium potatoes, chopped
1 tablespoon oregano
1 1/2 teaspoons salt
1/2 teaspoon pepper
12 small sweet cherry peppers, chopped
1 tablespoon capers, drained
6 bay leaves
3 cups water
1 cup dry sherry (optional)

Combine the conch with water to cover in a stockpot. Simmer for 30 minutes. Fry the bacon in a skillet until cooked through but not crisp. Add the bacon and bacon drippings to the conch. Add the onions, garlic, green pepper, tomato paste, tomato sauce, potatoes, oregano, salt, pepper, cherry peppers, capers, bay leaves and 3 cups water. Simmer until the potatoes are tender, stirring frequently to prevent sticking. Remove from the heat and let cool. Chill overnight. Reheat at serving time. Remove the bay leaves. Stir in the sherry.
Yield: 4 to 6 servings

Pat and Bill Braker

Everyday Bread

1 cup water   1 tablespoon honey   1 tablespoon vegetable oil
1 cup bread flour   1 cup whole wheat flour
1/2 cup rolled oats   1 tablespoon wheat bran
1 teaspoon salt   1 teaspoon dry yeast
1 teaspoon lecithin granules   2 tablespoons millet
2 teaspoons brewer's yeast (optional)

Combine the water, honey and oil in a bread machine container.
Add the flours, oats, wheat bran, salt, dry yeast, lecithin, millet and brewer's yeast.
Set the machine using manufacturer's directions. May add up to
1 3/4 teaspoons additional dry yeast for desired consistency.
Yield: 1 loaf

Julie Scheier, R.D.

Irish Soda Bread

1 (15-ounce) package raisins
6 cups flour   2 teaspoons baking soda
2 teaspoons baking powder
1 1/2 teaspoons cream of tartar   1 cup sugar
1 quart buttermilk   1/4 cup melted margarine

Soak the raisins in water in a small bowl for 10 minutes; drain and set aside. Sift the flour,
baking soda and baking powder into a large bowl. Add the cream of tartar, sugar and
buttermilk, mixing well. Stir in the raisins. Shape the dough into 4 equal portions. Place in
4 greased 9-inch loaf pans. Drizzle the margarine over the loaves. Bake at 350 degrees for
45 minutes. Cool in the pans for 5 minutes; remove to a wire rack to cool completely.
Yield: 4 loaves

Karen McDonnell

A diver hand-feeds the sea turtle in the
Coral Reef Exhibit in the center of the Aquarium.

Banana Bread

2 cups sifted flour $^2/_3$ cup sugar
1 tablespoon baking powder   1 teaspoon salt
$^1/_2$ cup semisweet chocolate chips   2 medium bananas, mashed
2 eggs, beaten $^1/_3$ cup vegetable oil

Sift the flour, sugar, baking powder and salt into a large bowl. Add the chocolate chips. Beat the bananas, eggs and oil in a small bowl. Add to the dry ingredients, stirring until moistened. Pour into a greased loaf pan. Bake at 350 degrees for 1 hour or until loaf tests done. Cool in the pan on a wire rack for 10 minutes. Invert onto serving plate.

Yield: 1 loaf

C. D. Abarbanell

Strawberry-Walnut Bread

1 cup finely chopped walnuts   3 cups flour
1 teaspoon baking soda $1^1/_2$ teaspoons cinnamon
$^1/_2$ teaspoon salt $^1/_4$ teaspoon ground nutmeg
4 eggs, beaten   2 cups sugar
$1^1/_2$ cups mashed strawberries
1 cup mashed bananas   1 cup vegetable oil

Sprinkle equal amounts of the chopped walnuts into 2 greased and floured loaf pans. Combine the flour, baking soda, cinnamon, salt and nutmeg in a large bowl. Mix the eggs, sugar, strawberries, bananas and oil in a medium bowl. Add to the dry ingredients, stirring until moistened. Pour into the prepared pans. Bake at 350 degrees for 1 hour or until loaves test tone. Cool in the pans for 10 minutes; remove to a wire rack to cool completely.

Yield: 2 loaves

Michelle Zaversnik

Carrot Muffins

2 cups flour
2 teaspoons baking soda
2 teaspoons cinnamon
1 1/2 cups sugar   2 teaspoons salt
2 (8-ounce) jars baby food carrots
1/2 cup vegetable oil
4 eggs, beaten
1/2 cup chopped nuts (optional)

Combine the flour, baking soda, cinnamon, sugar and salt in a large bowl. Beat the carrots, oil and eggs in a medium bowl. Add to the dry ingredients, stirring until moistened. Fold in the nuts. Pour into paper-lined muffin cups. Bake at 375 degrees for 18 to 20 minutes or until muffins test done. May prepare as bread by baking in a loaf pan for 55 to 60 minutes.
Yield: 24 muffins

Becky Bartosz

Whipped Cream Biscuits

1 1/2 cups flour
3/4 teaspoon salt
4 teaspoons baking powder
1 cup heavy cream, whipped

Combine the flour, salt and baking powder in a large bowl. Fold in the whipped cream until a stiff dough forms. Turn out onto a floured surface; knead lightly. Roll out to a 1/2-inch thickness. Cut into 2-inch biscuits. Place 1 inch apart on an ungreased baking sheet. Bake at 425 degrees for 10 to 12 minutes or until golden brown.
Yield: 16 biscuits

Mrs. William N. Sick

Grandma Cyrnek's Kolacky

1 cup butter, softened
16 ounces cream cheese, softened
2 cups flour   1 (12-ounce) can fruit filling   Confectioners' sugar

Cream the butter and cream cheese in a mixer bowl until light and fluffy. Sift the
flour into the mixture, stirring well. Turn out onto a floured surface. Roll out thinly with a
floured rolling pin. Cut out with a round cutter. Place the rounds on a nonstick baking sheet.
Make an indention in the center of each round; fill with the fruit filling. Bake at 400 degrees
for 12 to 15 minutes or until golden brown. Cool on a wire rack. Sprinkle with
confectioners' sugar before serving. May use a variety of fruit fillings.
Yield: 30 to 36 servings

Mary H. Martinez

Pull-Apart Rolls

3 tablespoons melted margarine
1 tablespoon onion flakes   2 teaspoons dillseeds
1/4 teaspoon celery seeds   1 teaspoon poppy seeds
1 (10-count) can biscuits
1/4 cup grated Parmesan cheese

Grease an 8-inch round pan with the margarine. Mix the onion flakes, dillseeds, celery
seeds and poppy seeds in a small bowl. Sprinkle evenly over the bottom of the pan.
Separate the biscuits and cut into quarters. Coat with the cheese. Arrange in a single layer
in the prepared pan. Sprinkle with any remaining cheese. Bake at 400 degrees for 15 to
18 minutes or until browned. Turn out onto a serving plate and serve immediately.
Yield: 6 to 8 servings

Pat Leverick

Caramel Pecan Rolls

3 envelopes dry yeast
$^1/_2$ cup lukewarm water
1 cup shortening
$^3/_4$ cup sugar
2 teaspoons salt
1 cup boiling water
4 eggs, beaten
$7^1/_2$ cups flour
1 cup cold water
2 cups chopped pecans
1 cup melted butter
$^1/_4$ cup lukewarm water
2 cups firmly packed brown sugar
3 tablespoons butter, softened
$1^1/_2$ cups sugar
$4^1/_2$ teaspoons cinnamon

Dissolve the yeast in $^1/_2$ cup lukewarm water. Beat the shortening, $^3/_4$ cup
sugar and salt in a large bowl. Add the boiling water, stirring well. Let cool slightly. Stir in
the yeast and eggs. Add the flour and cold water alternately to the mixture,
beating well after each addition. Grease the surface of the dough and let stand, covered,
for 8 to 10 hours. Spoon the pecans evenly into the cups of 3 muffin pans.
Combine the melted butter, $^1/_4$ cup lukewarm water and brown sugar in a small bowl,
mixing well. Pour over the pecans. Divide the dough into 3 portions. Roll out
on a floured surface into three 12x20-inch rectangles. Spread each rectangle with the
softened butter. Sprinkle evenly with a mixture of $1^1/_2$ cups sugar and cinnamon.
Roll up as for a jelly roll from the long edge. Cut each roll into 12 slices. Place cut side
down in the prepared muffin cups. Let rise, covered, in a warm place until doubled in bulk.
Bake at 375 degrees for 20 to 25 minutes or until golden brown.
Yield: 36 rolls

Marjorie Cochlan

Filled Danish Pastries with Confectioners' Sugar Icing

1 1/2 cups butter, softened
1/3 cup sifted flour
2 envelopes dry yeast or 2 yeast cakes
1/4 cup lukewarm water
1 cup milk, scalded
1/4 cup sugar
1/2 teaspoon salt
1 egg, beaten
4 cups sifted flour
Almond or Cream Cheese Filling
Confectioners' Sugar Icing

Cream the butter and 1/3 cup flour in a mixer bowl. Spread between 2 sheets of waxed paper to form a 6x12-inch rectangle. Chill thoroughly. Dissolve the yeast in the water. Combine the milk, sugar and salt in a large bowl; cool slightly. Stir in the yeast and egg. Add the flour gradually, stirring until a soft dough forms. Knead on a floured surface for 5 minutes or until the dough is smooth and elastic. Roll out on a floured surface into a 14-inch square. Place the chilled butter mixture on half of the square. Fold over the other half of the dough, sealing edges. Roll out on a floured surface into a 12x20-inch rectangle. Chill before proceeding if the butter softens. Fold into thirds, making 3 layers. Roll out into a 12x20-inch rectangle. Repeat the folding and rolling process twice. Chill for 30 minutes. Shape the dough into pastries. Place on an ungreased baking sheet. Let rise, covered, for 1 hour or until doubled in bulk. Bake at 450 degrees for 8 minutes. Trim with almond filling or cream cheese filling, or your favorite jelly or jam. Spread Confectioners' Sugar Icing over the top of each pastry. Let stand until set.

Filled Danish Pastry with Confectioners' Sugar Icing

(continued)

For the almond filling:
¹/₄ cup butter, softened
¹/₄ cup confectioners' sugar
¹/₄ cup ground almonds

Cream the butter and confectioners' sugar in a mixer bowl.
Stir in the almonds.

For the cream cheese filling:
16 ounces cream cheese, softened
1 egg yolk
1 cup sugar
1 teaspoon vanilla extract

Cream the cream cheese, egg yolk, sugar and vanilla
in a mixer bowl until light and fluffy.

For the confectioners' sugar icing:
2 cups sifted confectioners' sugar
Milk or light cream
1 teaspoon vanilla extract
Dash of salt

Mix the confectioners' sugar with 1 tablespoon of milk at a time
until of desired consistency. Stir in the vanilla and salt.
Yield: 36 pastries

Laris Gross

Blueberry Coffee Cake

4 cups flour   1 cup sugar
1 tablespoon plus 2 teaspoons baking powder
1/2 cup melted margarine   1 1/2 cups milk   2 eggs
4 cups blueberries   1 3/4 cups packed brown sugar
1 tablespoon cinnamon   1 cup melted butter

Combine the flour, sugar, baking powder, margarine, milk and eggs in a mixer bowl; beat well. Fold in the blueberries. Spread half the batter in a greased 9x13-inch baking pan. Mix the brown sugar, cinnamon and butter in a small bowl. Spread half the cinnamon mixture over the batter in the prepared baking pan. Cover with the remaining batter and top with the remaining cinnamon mixture. Bake at 350 degrees for 40 to 45 minutes or until browned.

Yield: 15 servings

Michelle Zaversnik

Gooey Butter Coffee Cake

1/2 cup melted butter   2 eggs, beaten
1 (2-layer) package butter cake mix   8 ounces cream cheese, softened
2 eggs, beaten   1 teaspoon vanilla extract
1 pound confectioners' sugar

Combine the butter, 2 eggs and cake mix in a bowl, mixing well. Pour into an ungreased 9x13-inch baking pan. Cream the cream cheese, 2 eggs, vanilla and confectioners' sugar in a mixer bowl until light and fluffy. Spread evenly over the batter. Bake at 350 degrees for 35 to 40 minutes or until browned. May dust with additional confectioners' sugar when cooled.

Yield: 15 servings

Mrs. G. Robert Muehlhauser

Diane's Coffee Cake

4 eggs   1 cup sour cream
1 (2-layer) package yellow cake mix $^2/_3$ cup vegetable oil
1 (3-ounce) package vanilla instant pudding mix
$^1/_2$ cup milk $^1/_2$ cup chopped pecans
$^3/_4$ cup packed brown sugar   2 teaspoons cinnamon

Beat the eggs, sour cream and cake mix in a large bowl. Add the oil, pudding mix and milk, stirring well. Pour half the batter into a well-greased bundt pan. Mix the pecans, brown sugar and cinnamon in a small bowl. Sprinkle half the cinnamon mixture over the batter in the bundt pan. Cover with the remaining batter and top with the remaining cinnamon mixture. Swirl with a knife to marbleize. Bake at 350 degrees for 45 minutes. Let cool in the pan for 10 minutes. Invert onto a serving plate.

Yield: 15 servings

Diane Chiligiris

Jewish Coffee Cake

1 cup butter, softened   2 cups sugar   2 cups sour cream
1 tablespoon baking soda   4 eggs   2 teaspoons vanilla extract
3 cups flour   2 teaspoons baking powder
$^1/_2$ cup sugar $^1/_2$ cup chopped walnuts   2 teaspoons cinnamon

Cream the butter and 2 cups sugar in a mixer bowl until light and fluffy. Stir in the sour cream and baking soda. Beat in the eggs 1 at a time. Stir in the vanilla, flour and baking powder. Mix the remaining ingredients in a small bowl. Stir half the cinnamon mixture into the batter. Pour into a greased 9x13-inch baking pan. Sprinkle with the remaining cinnamon mixture. Bake at 350 degrees for 45 minutes.

Yield: 15 servings

Roland J. Barnes

Cinnamon Loaf

$^1/_2$ cup butter or margarine, softened
1 cup sugar
2 eggs
1 teaspoon vanilla extract
1 cup sour cream
$^1/_4$ cup milk
2 cups flour
1$^1/_2$ teaspoons baking powder
1 teaspoon baking soda
$^1/_2$ teaspoon salt
$^1/_2$ cup sugar
2 tablespoons cinnamon

Cream the butter and 1 cup sugar in a mixer bowl until light and fluffy.
Add the eggs and vanilla; beat well. Add the sour cream and milk, beating until smooth.
Combine the flour, baking powder, baking soda and salt in a medium bowl. Stir
into the creamed mixture. Pour half the batter into a greased 5x9-inch loaf pan.
Mix $^1/_2$ cup sugar and cinnamon in a small bowl. Sprinkle $^3/_4$ of the cinnamon
mixture over the batter in the loaf pan. Cover with the remaining batter. Cut through the
batter with a knife to swirl, but avoid scraping the bottom of the pan. Sprinkle with the
remaining cinnamon mixture. Bake at 350 degrees for 1 hour. Cool in the pan for
10 minutes; remove to a wire rack to cool completely.
Yield: 10 servings

Michelle Zaversnik

Basic Crepes

1 cup flour   ½ teaspoon salt   2 eggs, beaten
1 cup milk   ¼ cup sugar
2 tablespoons chopped fresh mint leaves   2 tablespoons melted butter

Pour the flour into a bowl; make a well in the center. Add the salt and eggs. Pour in the milk gradually, whisking until smooth. Stir in the sugar and mint. Chill for 1 hour. Let stand to come to room temperature. Stir in the melted butter. Warm a greased crepe pan or a 7-inch nonstick skillet over low heat. Ladle 3 tablespoons of the batter into the pan, tilting pan to spread the batter over the surface. Cook until the bottom is browned. Turn and cook just until set. Continue until batter is used up, adding butter to the skillet as needed. Serve immediately. May store in the freezer by stacking the cooked crepes browned side down between sheets of waxed paper and tightly wrapping with plastic wrap or foil.

Yield: 16 servings

Linda Wilson

Whole Wheat Yogurt Pancakes

1 cup whole wheat flour   ⅓ cup all-purpose flour   1 teaspoon baking powder
1 teaspoon baking soda   2 tablespoons sugar   1 teaspoon salt
1 egg, beaten   ¾ cup milk   ½ cup yogurt
1 teaspoon vinegar   1 tablespoon melted butter   Vegetable oil for frying

Combine the flours, baking powder, baking soda, sugar and salt in a large bowl. Beat the egg, milk, yogurt and vinegar in a bowl. Stir into the dry ingredients. Add the butter, mixing well. Heat the oil on a griddle over high heat. Pour a small amount of the batter onto the griddle. Cook for 1 to 2 minutes; turn. Cook for 30 to 60 seconds longer. Repeat with remaining batter. Serve with fruit, applesauce, maple syrup, sliced bananas or wheat germ.

Yield: 8 to 10 servings

Richard Drews

Santa Fe Super Chief French Toast

This was one of the favorite items on the dining cars of the Super Chief and Chief trains of the Santa Fe Railway. Tastes even better when served at 90 miles per hour traveling through Southwestern Indian country.

3 ($3/4$-inch-thick) slices of bread, crusts trimmed
4 eggs, beaten   1 cup light cream or half-and-half
$1/4$ teaspoon salt   Vegetable oil for frying   Confectioners' sugar

Slice the bread diagonally to form 2 triangles. Beat the eggs, cream and salt in a bowl. Dip the bread into the mixture. Heat $1/2$ inch oil in an electric skillet to 325 degrees. Fry the bread until golden brown on each side, turning once. Drain on paper towels. Sprinkle with confectioners' sugar and serve with applesauce, jelly or maple syrup.

Yield: 3 servings

John Shedd Reed

Brunch Casserole

8 slices white bread, cubed $3/4$ cup melted butter
2 cups shredded cheese   2 cups thawed frozen chopped broccoli
2 cups cubed cooked ham   4 eggs
2 cups milk   Salt and pepper to taste

Toss the bread cubes with the melted butter. Layer half the bread, half the cheese, half the broccoli and all of the ham in a 9x13-inch baking pan sprayed with nonstick cooking spray. Layer the remaining broccoli, cheese and bread over layers. Beat the eggs, milk, salt and pepper in a small bowl. Pour over the layers. Chill, covered, for 8 to 10 hours. Bake at 350 degrees for 1 hour or until puffed and browned.

Yield: 6 to 8 servings

Louise Kuca

Cheese Enchiladas

1 pound ground beef   1 (8-ounce) can tomato sauce
¼ cup water   Salt and pepper to taste
Chili powder, thyme and ground cumin to taste
1 (8-ounce) package Velveeta cheese
1 (12-count) package corn tortilla shells
Vegetable oil   1 large onion, chopped

Cook the ground beef in a skillet, stirring until crumbly. Drain and set aside.
Mix the tomato sauce, water, salt, pepper, chili powder, thyme and cumin in a small bowl;
set aside. Cut part of the cheese into 12 slices; shred the remaining cheese. Heat the
tortilla shells in hot oil in a skillet for 3 seconds. Layer 1 slice of the cheese and equal
amounts of the ground beef and onion in each shell. Arrange in a 9x13-inch baking
dish. Pour the tomato sauce mixture over the shells. Top with the shredded cheese.
Bake at 325 degrees for 20 to 25 minutes or until the cheese is melted.
Yield: 12 servings

Angela Rossdeutcher

Spanokopita

12 sheets phyllo dough, thawed   Melted butter or margarine
3 pounds frozen chopped spinach, thawed
4 eggs   12 ounces feta cheese, crumbled

Spread 6 sheets of the dough with butter. Arrange in a buttered 9x13-inch baking pan.
Combine the spinach, eggs and cheese in a bowl, mixing well. Spread over the dough.
Top with the remaining sheets of dough, buttering each one generously. Seal the edges.
Bake at 375 degrees for 45 to 60 minutes or until puffed and browned.
Yield: 12 servings

Nan Graves

Sandwich Loaf

4 (5-ounce) cans chopped cooked chicken (about 3 cups)
1/4 cup chopped celery
1/2 teaspoon salt   1 tablespoon lemon juice
1/3 cup mayonnaise
3 cups ground cooked ham (about 1 pound)
1/3 cup pickle relish
2 tablespoons prepared mustard
2 tablespoons light brown sugar
1/2 cup mayonnaise
12 hard-cooked eggs, coarsely chopped
4 teaspoons capers, drained
1 teaspoon salt   1 tablespoon cider vinegar
2/3 cup mayonnaise
2 (2- to 3-pound) loaves unsliced white bread, crusts trimmed
32 ounces cream cheese, softened
1 cup milk

Mix the chicken, celery, 1/2 teaspoon salt, lemon juice and 1/3 cup mayonnaise
in a bowl; set aside. Mix the ham, pickle relish, mustard, brown sugar and 1/2 cup
mayonnaise in a bowl; set aside. Mix the eggs, capers, 1 teaspoon salt, vinegar and
2/3 cup mayonnaise in a bowl; set aside. Slice the bread loaves lengthwise into four
1/2-inch-thick sections. Cover the bread with a damp cloth. To assemble the loaf,
alternate layers of the bread, chicken salad, bread, ham salad, bread and egg salad
until all ingredients are used. Wrap with waxed paper and cover with a damp towel. Chill
for 8 to 10 hours. Place on a serving platter. Beat the cream cheese and milk in a mixer
bowl until light and fluffy. Reserve 1/2 cup cream cheese mixture. Place the loaf on a
serving platter. Frost the loaf carefully with the remaining cream cheese mixture.
Press the reserved cream cheese mixture through a pastry bag to decorate the loaf.
May tint with food coloring. Garnish with sprigs of watercress.
Yield: 32 servings

Barbara J. Stockton

Shrimp and Eggs

6 eggs
1/4 cup milk
2 to 3 drops of Tabasco sauce
2 to 3 drops of Pick-a-Pepper sauce
1 pound fresh shrimp, chopped into 1/2-inch pieces

Beat the eggs, milk, Tabasco sauce and Pick-a-Pepper sauce in a bowl; set aside.
Sauté the shrimp in a skillet until pink. Pour in the eggs.
Cook over medium heat until cooked through.
Yield: 10 servings

Linda Wilson

Chunky Cheese Soufflé

12 cups dry French bread cubes
Olive oil for frying
4 eggs, beaten   4 cups milk
8 ounces Swiss cheese, shredded
1 tablespoon prepared hot mustard
Chopped tomatoes
Sliced mushrooms

Brown the bread cubes in olive oil in a large skillet; set aside. Beat the eggs,
milk, cheese and mustard in a large bowl. Stir in the bread cubes, adding more milk
if needed to cover. Chill, covered, for 8 to 10 hours. Stir in the tomatoes and
mushrooms. Pour into a 9x13-inch baking pan. Bake at 325 degrees for 1 hour or until
puffed and browned. Garnish with chopped parsley or basil.
Yield: 12 servings

Nan Graves

Chicken Soufflé

4 cups chopped cooked chicken
1 cup chopped green bell pepper
1 cup chopped celery
1 cup chopped onion
1 cup mayonnaise
1 1/2 teaspoons salt
1 1/2 teaspoons pepper
12 slices white bread, crusts trimmed, cubed
4 eggs, beaten
3 cups milk
2 (10-ounce) cans cream of mushroom soup
1 cup shredded Cheddar cheese

Combine the chicken, green pepper, celery, onion, mayonnaise, salt and
pepper in a bowl; mix well. Arrange half the bread cubes in a greased 9x13-inch
baking pan. Top with the chicken mixture and the remaining bread. Beat the
eggs and milk in a bowl. Pour over the layers. Chill, covered, for 8 to 10 hours.
Spread the soup over the top. Sprinkle with the cheese.
Bake at 350 degrees for 1 hour.
Yield: 8 to 10 servings

Mrs. Robert D. Krebs

PASTA and SAUCES

Pasta and Sauces
Kugel

Kugel is a traditional Jewish dish. This one usually gets raves.
"Delicious, Bubbe" is the shout of my grandchildren.

24 ounces yolk-free wide noodles
1/2 cup melted margarine
3 eggs, beaten
3/4 cup egg substitute
2 cups fat-free sour cream
2 cups fat-free cottage cheese
3/4 cup milk
1/2 teaspoon salt
1/2 cup sugar
7 ounces golden raisins
1 cup cornflake crumbs
1 cup brown sugar
1/4 cup melted margarine

Cook the noodles using package directions; drain well. Combine with the
margarine in a bowl, tossing to coat. Stir in the eggs, egg substitute, sour cream, cottage
cheese, milk, salt, sugar and raisins. Pour into a nonstick 10x15-inch baking pan.
Toss the cornflake crumbs, brown sugar and margarine in a small bowl. Sprinkle over the
noodles. Chill, covered, for 8 to 10 hours. Bake at 350 degrees for 1 hour.
Yield: 15 servings

Evelyn Pinsof

A child enjoys the view of a Pacific white-sided dolphin from
Shedd Aquarium's underwater viewing area.

Sarasota Noodles

8 ounces very fine noodles
12 ounces cream cheese, softened
8 ounces cottage cheese, drained
2 tablespoons finely chopped onion
2 tablespoons Worcestershire sauce
16 ounces sour cream
1 1/2 teaspoons salt
1 teaspoon sugar
1 teaspoon dry mustard
1 teaspoon MSG (Accent)
2 teaspoons oregano
1 1/2 teaspoons garlic powder
1/2 teaspoon pepper
1 cup freshly grated Parmesan cheese

Cook the noodles using package directions; drain. Combine with the cream
cheese, cottage cheese, onion, Worcestershire sauce and sour cream in a bowl; mix well.
Spoon into a 2-quart baking dish. Mix the salt, sugar, mustard, MSG, oregano, garlic
powder, pepper and Parmesan cheese in a small bowl. Sprinkle evenly over the noodles.
Bake at 375 degrees for 45 to 60 minutes or until browned and bubbly.
Yield: 8 servings

Jennifer Foskit

Noodle Casserole

This dish is always a big success because it's just a little different.

1 (16-ounce) package fine noodles
1 cup butter
2 cups uncooked quick-cooking rice
2 (10-ounce) cans onion soup   2 (10-ounce) cans chicken broth
1 tablespoon soy sauce
1 (8-ounce) can sliced water chestnuts
1 cup water

Sauté the noodles in butter in a large skillet until golden brown. Combine
with the rice, onion soup, chicken broth, soy sauce, water chestnuts
and water in a large bowl, mixing well. Spoon into a 9x12-inch baking dish.
Bake at 350 degrees for 45 minutes.
Yield: 12 servings

Renée S. Crown

Noodles with Tuna and Mushrooms

My two children, Alex and Stephanie Lauder, invented this recipe.

8 ounces noodles or other pasta
1 (10-ounce) can golden mushroom soup
1 (6-ounce) can tuna, drained

Cook the pasta using package directions. Drain well and set aside.
Warm the soup in a saucepan over low heat. Stir in the noodles and the tuna,
mixing well. Cook until heated through. Serve immediately.
Yield: 4 servings

Vera Terec

Chicken Ricotta Pasta

2 whole chicken breasts, boned, skinned
1 onion, sliced
2 to 3 whole peppercorns
2 (4-ounce) cans whole green chiles, drained
1 1/2 cups ricotta cheese
1 1/2 cups shredded Monterey Jack cheese
Salt and freshly ground pepper to taste
1 (15-ounce) can herb-flavored tomato sauce
8 ounces pasta, cooked

Combine the chicken, onion and peppercorns with water to cover in a medium skillet. Simmer over medium heat for 8 to 10 minutes or until the chicken is cooked through. Rinse the chiles and slice lengthwise. Place half of the chiles in a buttered 8-inch square baking dish. Cover with 1/2 cup of the ricotta cheese. Sprinkle with 1/2 of the Monterey Jack cheese. Arrange the undrained chicken mixture over the cheese. Season with salt and pepper. Layer with the remaining ricotta cheese, Monterey Jack cheese and chiles. Pour the tomato sauce over the layers. Bake at 375 degrees for 20 to 30 minutes.

Cut into four portions and serve over the pasta.

Yield: 4 servings

Louise M. Flannery

Pasta and Sauces
Italian Spaghetti

My mother made this for us. It was always one of the dishes
at Christmas time. I make it now for my family.

1 pound ground round
1 teaspoon salt
$1/8$ teaspoon pepper
Garlic salt to taste
$1/4$ cup chopped onion
2 tablespoons vegetable oil
1 pound Italian or other sausage, cut into $2^1/2$-inch pieces
2 to 3 pork neck bones
2 (6-ounce) cans tomato paste
1 (28-ounce) can whole tomatoes
1 teaspoon sugar
$1/4$ teaspoon nutmeg
$1/2$ teaspoon oregano
$1/4$ cup chopped parsley
2 tablespoons celery flakes
$1/4$ cup grated cheese
1 cup water
16 ounces spaghetti

Brown the ground round in a large skillet, stirring until crumbly; drain.
Season with salt, pepper and garlic salt. Sauté the onion in oil in a large stockpot until
tender. Add the cooked ground round, sausage, neck bones, tomato paste,
tomatoes, sugar, nutmeg, oregano, parsley, celery flakes, cheese and water.
Bring to a boil; reduce heat. Simmer for 2 to $2^1/2$ hours, stirring
occasionally and skimming the top of the sauce every 30 minutes. Add additional
water for desired consistency. Cook the spaghetti using package
directions; drain. Ladle the sauce over the spaghetti to serve.
Yield: 8 servings

Vera Szymonik

Pasta with Cherry Tomatoes and Shrimp Sauce

2 to 3 cloves of garlic
$1/4$ cup olive oil
6 cups cherry tomatoes
$1/2$ cup chicken bouillon
$1/2$ cup dry white wine
$1/4$ cup chopped fresh parsley
8 ounces shrimp, unpeeled
16 ounces linguini

Sauté the garlic in the oil in a large deep skillet until tender. Cut the tomatoes into halves. Add to the skillet with the bouillon and wine. Simmer over medium-low heat for 10 minutes. Add the parsley and the shrimp. Simmer for 3 to 5 minutes longer or until the shrimp are cooked through. Cook the linguini al dente using package directions; drain. Combine with the sauce in a large bowl, tossing to coat.

Yield: 4 servings

Michael Delfini

Pasta and Sauces
Linsey's Rotini

1 pound breakfast sausage
1 clove of garlic, pressed or chopped
1 tablespoon olive oil
10 large mushrooms, sliced
1 (10-ounce) package frozen chopped spinach, thawed, drained
1 (16-ounce) can chopped tomatoes, drained
16 ounces rotini pasta
Grated Parmesan cheese to taste

Cook the sausage in a large skillet until browned, stirring until crumbly;
drain well and set aside. Sauté the garlic in olive oil in a small skillet. Add the
mushrooms. Sauté until lightly browned; drain. Combine with the sausage, spinach
and tomatoes in a saucepan. Simmer until heated through, stirring occasionally.
Cook the rotini using package directions; drain well. Combine with
the sausage mixture in a large bowl, tossing to coat.
Sprinkle with cheese before serving.
Yield: 4 servings

Linsey A. Foster

Swiss Mountain Pasta

Kurt and I first enjoyed this dish in a small village in Switzerland. Upon our arrival home I attempted to duplicate the dish. This comes close.

2 large baking potatoes, peeled, cubed
16 ounces ziti, penne or other tubular pasta
1 large Spanish onion, thinly sliced
1/2 cup butter
16 ounces Swiss cheese, shredded

Place potatoes with a small amount of water in a microwave-safe dish. Microwave on High for 10 minutes. Drain and set aside. Cook the pasta al dente using package directions. Drain and place in a large bowl. Sauté the onion in butter in a skillet. Combine with the pasta, potatoes and Swiss cheese, mixing well. Spoon into an ungreased 2-quart baking dish. Bake at 350 degrees for 20 to 30 minutes or until lightly browned. May crumble crisp-fried bacon over the top before serving.
Yield: 8 servings

Kathleen Stocker

Chicken Pesto Lasagna

This is a very easy and very tasty reduced-fat version of lasagna.

4 boneless skinless chicken breast halves
Salt to taste
3 to 4 celery tops
1 small onion, cut into quarters
2 cups grated zucchini, drained
3/4 cup Basic Pesto Sauce (page 101)
1 1/2 cups part skim milk ricotta cheese
1/2 cup grated Parmesan cheese
12 ounces lasagna noodles
1 (28-ounce) jar spaghetti sauce
8 ounces part skim milk mozzarella cheese, shredded or sliced

Rinse the chicken and pat dry. Place the chicken in a large saucepan with water to cover. Add salt, celery and onion; cover. Bring to a boil; remove from heat. Let stand for 25 minutes; drain. Chop or shred the chicken. Squeeze the moisture from the zucchini with a paper towel. Mix the chicken with the zucchini and pesto in a bowl. Combine the ricotta and Parmesan cheeses in a small bowl. Cook the lasagna noodles using package directions. Spread 1 cup of the spaghetti sauce in a 9x13-inch baking pan. Layer with 3 noodles, 1/2 of the cheese mixture and 1/2 of the chicken mixture. Repeat the layers. Top with the remaining noodles. Cover with the remaining spaghetti sauce and mozzarella cheese. Bake at 350 degrees for 30 minutes.
Yield: 6 to 8 servings

Jeanne Landreth

Vegetarian Lasagna

I have altered this twenty-year-old recipe to make use of the zucchini I harvested this summer.

8 lasagna noodles
2 eggs, beaten
8 ounces ricotta cheese
2 tablespoons vegetable oil
2 cloves of garlic, minced
1 medium onion, chopped
1 pound zucchini, chopped
1/2 cup Gran-burger (vegetable protein granules)
1 teaspoon salt
1/4 teaspoon pepper
1/2 teaspoon rosemary
1 tablespoon minced parsley
2 (6-ounce) cans tomato paste
1 1/2 cups hot water
12 ounces mozzarella cheese, sliced
1/4 cup grated Parmesan cheese

Cook the lasagna noodles using package directions; drain. Mix the eggs
and ricotta cheese in a small bowl; set aside. Heat the oil in a large deep skillet.
Sauté the garlic and onion in the skillet until tender. Add the zucchini, Gran-burger, salt,
pepper, rosemary and parsley. Cook for 10 minutes. Add a mixture of the tomato
paste and hot water. Simmer for 5 minutes. Spread a thin layer of the mixture in a 9x13-inch
baking dish. Layer with half the noodles, all the ricotta cheese mixture and half the
mozzarella cheese. Top with half the zucchini sauce, the remaining noodles, the remaining
zucchini sauce and the remaining mozzarella cheese. Sprinkle with Parmesan cheese. Bake
at 350 degrees for 30 minutes. Let stand for 10 minutes before serving.
Yield: 8 servings

C. D. Abarbanell

Pasta and Sauces
Fruit Chili Sauce

2 tablespoons mixed whole spices (cloves, nutmeg and allspice)
10 medium tomatoes, chopped
6 medium onions, chopped   8 pears, peeled, chopped
8 peaches, peeled, chopped
5 cups sugar   2 tablespoons salt
1 quart cider vinegar

Tie the spices in a small cheesecloth bag. Combine with the tomatoes, onions, pears, peaches, sugar, salt and vinegar in a large nonreactive saucepan. Bring to a boil, stirring constantly; reduce heat. Simmer for 2 to 3 hours or until thickened, stirring frequently to prevent sticking. Ladle into 6 sterilized pint jars, leaving 1/2-inch headspace. Seal with 2-piece lids. Process in a hot water bath for 10 minutes.
Yield: 6 pints

Laris Gross

Pasta and Sauces
Tom-A-Que Sauce

3 cups tomato sauce
1 medium onion, cut into quarters
2 cloves of garlic, crushed   1 tablespoon brown sugar
1 teaspoon hickory smoke extract
1/2 teaspoon Tabasco sauce
1 fresh chile pepper, seeded (optional)

Combine the tomato sauce, onion, garlic, brown sugar, smoke extract, Tabasco sauce and chile pepper in a blender container. Process at low speed for 3 minutes. Pour into a container and cover. Chill overnight before using. Excellent for shish kabob.
Yield: 3 cups

Thomas Appel

Bernaise Sauce

1/4 cup tarragon vinegar
1/4 cup dry white wine
1 tablespoon chopped shallots
1/2 teaspoon dried tarragon
3 egg yolks
2 tablespoons butter
Salt and pepper to taste
1/2 cup butter, melted

Combine the vinegar, wine, shallots and tarragon in a
small saucepan. Bring to a boil. Cook until the mixture is reduced by half.
Beat the egg yolks with 2 tablespoons butter in a double boiler
over hot water. Heat over low heat just until the butter has melted, stirring constantly.
Add the vinegar mixture gradually, stirring constantly. Stir in the
salt, pepper and 1/2 cup butter. Cook until thickened, stirring frequently.
Yield: 1 cup

Betsy Schroeder

Clam Sauce

1 (6-ounce) can clams   3 cloves of garlic, minced
3 tablespoons olive oil   1 tablespoon butter or margarine
1 teaspoon dry oregano, or 1/4 cup chopped fresh oregano
1/2 teaspoon freshly ground pepper   3/4 cup dry white wine
3 tablespoons butter or margarine   1/4 cup half-and-half (optional)
Salt and pepper to taste

Drain the clams, reserving the juice; set aside. Sauté the garlic in olive oil and 1 tablespoon
butter in a skillet for 1 to 2 minutes; do not brown the garlic. Add the oregano, pepper,
white wine and reserved clam juice. Cook over high heat until the mixture is reduced by
half; reduce heat. Add the clams, 3 tablespoons butter and half-and-half. Cook over low
heat until thickened, stirring frequently. Season with salt and pepper. Serve over linguini.

Yield: 1 cup

Richard Drews

Basic Pesto Sauce

2 cups fresh basil leaves   4 to 8 cloves of garlic
1 cup pine nuts or walnuts   1/2 to 1 cup olive oil
1 cup freshly grated Parmesan cheese   1/4 cup freshly grated Romano cheese
Salt and pepper to taste

Combine the basil, garlic and pine nuts in a food processor container fitted
with a steel blade. Begin processing, adding the oil in a thin steady stream. Add the
Parmesan and Romano cheeses, salt and pepper. Process until thickened.
Pour into a container and chill, covered, until needed. Serve at room temperature
over pasta or spread over slices of French bread, toasting to melt the cheese.

Yield: 2 cups

Barbara Stockton

Red Pepper Sauce

2 red bell peppers, chopped
2 tablespoons olive oil
2 cups coarsely chopped onions
2 teaspoons minced garlic
$1/2$ teaspoon red pepper flakes
1 cup chicken stock
$1/4$ cup chopped fresh basil
Salt and pepper to taste

Sauté the peppers in oil in a large skillet for 5 minutes. Add the onions, garlic
and pepper flakes. Sauté for 2 to 3 minutes. Add the chicken stock.
Simmer for 15 minutes, stirring occasionally. Pour into a food processor container.
Process on high until puréed. Pour back into the skillet. Add the basil,
salt and pepper. Simmer until heated through. May substitute yellow bell
peppers for a yellow sauce to serve over asparagus.
Yield: 5 cups

Betsy Schroeder

Neapolitan Meat Sauce

My best friend, who is Italian, made me vow never to tell her grandmother, a native of Naples, that she gave me her recipe from the "Old Country." This is the favorite recipe of my five grandchildren (now grown) and guests. I've made it for over thirty years.

4 pounds ground round
2 teaspoons salt
1 teaspoon oregano
1 teaspoon basil
1 large yellow onion, finely chopped
1 medium green bell pepper, finely chopped
4 large cloves of garlic, minced
1 tablespoon olive oil
1/2 teaspoon freshly ground pepper
2 (28-ounce) cans tomato purée
2 (28-ounce) cans crushed tomatoes in purée
1 (15-ounce) can tomato purée
1 (12-ounce) can tomato paste
2 cloves of garlic, crushed
2 teaspoons sugar

Brown the ground round with salt, oregano and basil in a large skillet, stirring until crumbly; drain well. Transfer to a large stockpot. Sauté the onion, green pepper and 4 cloves of garlic in olive oil in a skillet. Add to the ground round. Add the remaining ingredients; mix well. Bring to a slow boil; reduce heat to low. Simmer, covered, for 4 hours, stirring occasionally. Serve over any pasta.

Yield: 18 servings

Bonita Levin

Vegetable Marinara Sauce

I developed this recipe when our family decided to eat heart-healthy meals.

4 to 8 cloves of garlic, crushed
1 small onion, thinly sliced
White part of 1 large leek, thinly sliced
2 tablespoons olive oil
1 (16-ounce) can tomato paste
3 (28-ounce) cans tomato sauce
1 (28-ounce) can plum tomatoes
3/4 cup red wine
Sea salt and freshly ground black pepper to taste
1 tablespoon fresh chopped oregano
1 tablespoon fresh chopped thyme
1 tablespoon fresh chopped basil
8 ounces broccoli flowerets
8 ounces cauliflowerets
2 large red bell peppers, chopped
1 large green bell pepper, chopped
8 ounces white mushrooms, sliced into halves
2 small zucchini, sliced

Sauté the garlic, onion and leek in olive oil in a large stockpot until light golden brown. Add the tomato paste, tomato sauce, tomatoes, wine, salt and pepper. Bring to a boil; reduce heat to low. Simmer for 1 hour, stirring occasionally. Add the oregano, thyme and basil. Add additional wine or water for desired consistency. Steam the broccoli, cauliflowerets, bell peppers, mushrooms and zucchini in a steamer until tender-crisp. Add to the sauce mixture. Simmer for 15 minutes longer. May add 1/2 teaspoon sugar if the sauce is too acidic. Serve over pasta topped with freshly grated Parmesan cheese.
Yield: 8 to 10 servings

Elaine Klemen

Oriental Spiced Strip Steaks

This recipe combines my Chinese heritage, American upbringing and enjoyment of spicy foods. The blend of ginger, jalapeños and garlic rubbed on the steaks brings a combined flavor that crosses cultural borders. The roasted peppers add a colorful garnish to the meal. Add a glass of wine, and you've got an appealing meal for family or friends.

2 tablespoons julienned fresh ginger
1 tablespoon chopped fresh jalapeños
1 tablespoon chopped fresh garlic
4 (8-ounce) New York strip steaks, trimmed
1 tablespoon sesame seed oil
2 tablespoons teriyaki sauce
1 lemon
Freshly ground pepper to taste
1 green bell pepper, sliced
1 red bell pepper, sliced

Mix the ginger, jalapeños and garlic in a bowl. Rub the mixture over and into the steaks. Mix the oil and teriyaki sauce in a shallow glass dish. Add the steaks, turning to coat well. Squeeze the juice from the lemon over the steaks. Sprinkle with the pepper to taste. Marinate in the refrigerator for 3 hours to overnight. Remove the steaks from the marinade and place on a broiler pan. Broil for 3 minutes per side for rare, 4 minutes per side for medium or 5 minutes per side for well done. Top with the bell pepper slices during the last 4 minutes of cooking. Serve with a garden salad and rice pilaf.

Yield: 4 servings

Jimmy Nge

Intricate detailing decorates the brass front doors of the Aquarium.

107

Meats, Poultry, and Seafood
Super Beef Stroganoff

1/4 cup minced onion
1/2 cup butter
8 ounces mushrooms, sliced
1 pound round steak, cut into 1/2-inch strips
2 tablespoons flour
1/2 teaspoon salt
1/8 teaspoon pepper, or to taste
1/8 teaspoon garlic powder
1/2 teaspoon dry mustard
1 tablespoon tomato paste
1/2 cup consommé
1/2 cup dry white wine
1/2 cup sour cream
3 tablespoons sherry

Sauté the onion in the butter in a skillet for 10 minutes. Add the mushrooms.
Cook, covered, for 5 minutes. Remove the mushroom mixture to a bowl. Add the
steak strips to the skillet. Cook over low heat until browned. Stir in the
flour. Add the salt, pepper, garlic powder, dry mustard, mushroom mixture, tomato
paste, consommé and wine and mix well. Simmer for 1 hour or until the
steak is tender. Stir in the sour cream and sherry just before serving.

Yield: 4 servings

Maureen Murphy

Meats, Poultry, and Seafood
French Pot Roast

1 pot roast   French or Italian salad dressing
Minced onions   Minced green bell pepper

Marinate the roast in the salad dressing in a large bowl in the refrigerator overnight.
Remove the roast from the marinade and place in a roasting bag. Top with the
onions and green pepper. Tie the bag to enclose the roast and place in a roasting pan.
Bake at 350 degrees for 1 hour and 20 minutes or until the roast is tender.
Yield: 8 to 12 servings

Elaine Kasdan

Meats, Poultry, and Seafood
Tangy Texas Brisket

*This is a great recipe if you are having a party and want to spend more time with
your guests. The leftovers make great sandwiches, but it reheats well, too.*

1 (4- to 5-pound) beef brisket $^{1}/_{2}$ teaspoon salt
$^{1}/_{4}$ teaspoon garlic salt $^{1}/_{4}$ cup chopped onion
2 teaspoons BV   1 teaspoon liquid smoke
1 teaspoon pepper sauce   1 teaspoon MSG
$^{1}/_{2}$ teaspoon sugar $^{1}/_{4}$ cup soy sauce
$^{1}/_{4}$ cup Worcestershire sauce

Rub the brisket with the salt and garlic salt. Place in an ovenproof baking dish.
Combine the onion, BV, liquid smoke, pepper sauce, MSG, sugar, soy sauce and
Worcestershire sauce in a bowl and mix well. Pour over the brisket. Marinate, covered, in
the refrigerator for 24 hours, turning 4 times. Roast at 250 degrees for 6 to $6^{1}/_{2}$ hours or
until cooked to the desired degree of doneness. Make a gravy using the pan drippings.
Yield: 5 to 7 servings

Lorel M. Allseits

Beefy Chimichangas

1 pound lean ground beef
1/2 cup finely chopped onion
1 (16-ounce) can refried beans
2 teaspoons chili powder
1/2 teaspoon cumin
2 cloves of garlic, minced
3 (8-ounce) cans tomato sauce
10 to 12 (10-inch) flour tortillas
1 (4-ounce) can chopped green chiles, drained
1 canned jalapeño, chopped
Low-fat or fat-free margarine
1 1/2 cups shredded Cheddar or Monterey Jack cheese

Brown the ground beef in a large skillet, stirring until crumbly; drain well.
Stir in the onion, beans, chili powder, cumin, garlic and 1/2 cup of the tomato sauce. Spoon
1/3 cup of the ground beef mixture slightly off-center onto a tortilla. Fold the edge nearest
the filling up and over the filling, just until the filling is covered. Fold the opposite side
of the tortilla in to the center; roll up and secure with a wooden pick. Place in a
baking pan. Repeat with the remaining ground beef mixture and tortillas. Combine the
remaining tomato sauce, green chiles and jalapeño in a saucepan. Cook over
medium heat just until heated through. Brush the chimichangas with the margarine.
Bake at 500 degrees for 5 to 8 minutes or until browned. Pour the tomato sauce mixture
over the chimichangas. Sprinkle with the cheese. Bake until heated through.
Remove the wooden picks. Serve with low-fat sour cream.
Yield: 10 to 12 servings

Eileen E. Semeniuk

Meats, Poultry, and Seafood
Poor Boy Fillets

1 pound ground beef   1/4 cup grated Parmesan cheese
1 (2-ounce) can mushroom stems and pieces, drained
2 tablespoons finely chopped onion
2 tablespoons finely chopped green bell pepper
Partially cooked bacon slices

Pat the ground beef 1/3 inch thick on waxed paper. Shape into a 7x12-inch rectangle. Sprinkle with the cheese. Mix the mushroom pieces, onion and green pepper in a bowl. Spread over the ground beef. Roll up as for a jelly roll; cut into 1 1/2-inch slices. Wrap the edge of each slice with a bacon slice and secure with a wooden pick. Place the slices on a sheet of foil on a grill rack. Grill for 8 minutes per side or until cooked through.

Yield: 5 servings

Mrs. John G. Shedd

Meats, Poultry, and Seafood
Sloppy Joes

1 cup finely chopped onion
2 tablespoons olive oil
1 pound lean ground beef   1/2 cup catsup   1 (8-ounce) can tomato sauce
1/4 cup water   2 tablespoons red wine vinegar
1 tablespoon Worcestershire sauce   2 tablespoons dark brown sugar
1 teaspoon salt   Freshly ground pepper to taste
2 drops of Tabasco sauce (optional)   4 hamburger buns

Cook the onion in the olive oil in a 10- to 12-inch skillet until tender. Add the ground beef. Cook just until browned, stirring until crumbly; drain well. Mix the next 9 ingredients in a large bowl. Combine with the ground beef mixture in the skillet. Simmer over low heat for 20 to 25 minutes or until heated through, stirring frequently. Serve over the buns.

Yield: 4 servings

Jane McDonald

Italian Meatballs

1/2 cup crushed crackers
1/2 cup milk
1 pound lean ground beef or ground chuck
1 small onion, grated
1/8 teaspoon salt, or to taste
1 small onion, grated
3/4 cup water
3/4 cup catsup
2 tablespoons mustard
2 tablespoons wine vinegar
1/4 cup packed brown sugar

Mix the cracker crumbs and milk in a large bowl. Add the ground beef, 1 onion and salt and mix well. Shape into 1-inch balls. Pour enough water to measure 1/2 inch into a broiler pan. Place the meatballs on the broiler rack in the pan. Bake at 325 degrees for 1 hour, turning once. Bring the remaining onion, 3/4 cup water, catsup, mustard, vinegar and brown sugar to a boil in a saucepan. Simmer for 30 minutes. Add the meatballs. Marinate in the refrigerator for several hours to overnight; the sauce will thicken. Reheat slowly. May serve over favorite pasta.
Yield: 25 meatballs

Chari Giese

Pork Chops Drury Express

This excellent recipe takes care of your vegetable, too. A gallant railroad man, George Drury, gets the credit. Though it's just as simple as it sounds, the finished product seems more than the sum of its parts.

3 tablespoons flour
1 1/2 tablespoons grated Parmesan cheese
1 1/2 teaspoons salt
1/2 teaspoon dillweed
1/4 teaspoon pepper
4 to 6 lean pork chops
Vegetable oil for browning
2 medium onions, sliced
1/3 cup water
3 green zucchini, sliced
3 tablespoons grated Parmesan cheese
1/2 teaspoon paprika

Combine the flour, 1 1/2 tablespoons cheese, salt, dillweed and pepper in a
plastic bag. Add the pork chops, shaking to coat well. Heat the oil in a
large skillet. Add the pork chops, reserving the flour mixture. Cook until the pork
chops are browned. Arrange the onion slices over the pork chops. Add the water. Simmer,
covered, for 15 minutes. Add the zucchini. Mix the reserved flour mixture,
3 tablespoons cheese and paprika together. Sprinkle over the pork chops; do not stir.
Simmer, covered, for 25 minutes. Let stand for 10 minutes before serving.
Yield: 4 to 6 servings

Georgean Booras

Pork Chops à la Jennifer

6 pork chops
1 Spanish onion, cut into ¼-inch slices   1 green bell pepper, sliced
1 (10-ounce) can tomato soup   1 soup can water
Salt and pepper to taste

Brown the pork chops in a skillet. Arrange in a single layer in a shallow rectangular casserole or 9x13-inch baking pan. Top each pork chop with 1 onion slice and 1 green pepper slice. Mix the soup and water in a bowl. Pour over the pork chops. Season with the salt and pepper. Bake, covered, at 325 degrees for 1 hour and 15 minutes. Bake, uncovered, for 15 minutes longer. Serve with mashed potatoes.

Yield: 6 servings

Bernadette Linhart

Southern Pork Chops

4 large lean pork chops
1 tablespoon vegetable oil
4 thick onion slices   ¼ cup peanut butter
1 (10-ounce) can cream of mushroom soup
⅓ cup milk   1 teaspoon Worcestershire sauce
½ teaspoon salt (optional)
⅛ teaspoon freshly ground pepper

Brown the pork chops in the oil in a skillet; drain. Top each pork chop with an onion slice. Combine the peanut butter, soup, milk, Worcestershire sauce, salt and pepper in a bowl and mix well. Pour over the pork chops. Cook, covered, over low heat for 45 minutes or until the pork chops are tender. Serve with rice or noodles.

Yield: 4 servings

Cheryl Gosiewski

Meats, Poultry, and Seafood

Skewered Marinated Pork Tenderloin

1 cup chopped onion   1 clove of garlic, pressed
2 tablespoons ground coriander
2 tablespoons brown sugar
1/4 cup lemon juice   1/4 cup olive oil
1/4 cup vegetable oil   1/4 cup soy sauce
1/4 teaspoon red pepper
2 pounds pork tenderloin, cut into 1 1/2-inch cubes
2 red onions, cut into wedges
Fresh vegetables of your choice, cut to fit skewers

Combine the chopped onion, garlic, coriander, brown sugar, lemon juice,
olive oil, vegetable oil, soy sauce and red pepper in a large bowl. Add the tenderloin.
Marinate in the refrigerator overnight. Thread the tenderloin, red onions and other
vegetables onto skewers. Place on the grill rack. Grill for 7 minutes per side.
Yield: 8 to 12 servings

Mrs. Robert D. Krebs

Meats, Poultry, and Seafood

Teriyaki Pork Tenderloin

1/4 cup soy sauce   1 to 2 cloves of garlic, minced
2 tablespoons olive oil   2 tablespoons brown sugar
1 teaspoon grated ginger   1/2 teaspoon freshly ground pepper
2 (12-ounce) pork tenderloins

Whisk the soy sauce, garlic, olive oil, brown sugar, ginger and pepper in
a bowl until mixed. Pour over the pork in a shallow pan. Marinate in the refrigerator
for 6 to 7 hours. Place on the grill rack. Grill for 12 to 15 minutes or until cooked
through, turning frequently and basting with the marinade.
Yield: 6 to 8 servings

Kathy Kompare

Barbecued Ribs

3 to 4 pounds country-style pork ribs
Poultry seasoning and celery seeds to taste
Salt and pepper to taste
1 cup catsup
1 tablespoon Worcestershire sauce
1/4 cup A.1. steak sauce
1/2 teaspoon chili powder
2 tablespoons butter

Sprinkle both sides of the ribs with the poultry seasoning, celery seeds,
salt and pepper; rub into the meat. Place on the grill rack. Grill over gas or charcoal
for 20 minutes on 1 side and 15 minutes on the other. Bring the catsup, Worcestershire
sauce, steak sauce, chili powder and butter to a boil in a saucepan. Serve with the ribs.
Yield: 4 to 5 servings

Mrs. John G. Shedd

Meats, Poultry, and Seafood
Vic's Barn-Burner Choucroute Garni

2 large jars Bavarian-style sauerkraut
4 to 5 smoked boneless pork chops
2 smoked sausages, cut into 3-inch pieces
1 package white bratwurst, cut into halves
1 package knockwurst, cut into halves
4 cups (or more) water
$\frac{1}{2}$ cup sugar
Salt and pepper to taste
$\frac{1}{4}$ cup butter
4 to 5 tablespoons flour

Drain the sauerkraut; rinse in cold water and drain again. Alternate layers of the sauerkraut, pork chops, sausages, bratwurst and knockwurst in a very large stockpot, ending with the sauerkraut. Add the water, sugar, salt and pepper. Bring to a boil; reduce the heat immediately. Simmer, covered, for 1 hour or until the mixture is cooked through and the sausages have started to burst, stirring occasionally and adding additional water if needed. May serve at this point or continue and make a roux. Remove the meats and keep warm. Remove 2 to 3 cups of the cooking liquid to a bowl and keep warm. Melt the butter in a small skillet. Add the flour as the foam subsides, whisking vigorously to remove any lumps. Cook briefly. Add to the hot cooking liquid, whisking to remove any lumps and adding additional liquid if the mixture becomes too thick. Add to the stockpot and whisk with the sauerkraut until the mixture is of the desired thickness. Add the meats or serve the meats and sauerkraut separately.

Yield: 6 servings

Vicky Stumpf

Gemelli with Escarole, Beans and Sausage

1 pound Italian sausage, casing removed
1 pound gemelli or fusilli pasta
2 tablespoons extra-virgin olive oil
1 to 2 cloves of garlic, thinly sliced
1 head escarole, coarsely chopped
1 (19-ounce) can cannellini beans
Freshly grated Parmesan cheese to taste
Freshly ground pepper to taste

Cook the sausage in a large skillet for 10 minutes or until browned, breaking
up with a fork. Remove with a slotted spoon. Drain and rinse the skillet. Cook the pasta
using the package directions until al dente; drain well, reserving 1 to 1½ cups cooking
liquid. Heat the olive oil in the skillet. Add the garlic. Sauté for 2 minutes. Add the escarole.
Sauté for 5 minutes or until the escarole is wilted. Add the undrained beans. Cook for
3 minutes or until heated through. Add the pasta and enough of the reserved liquid to keep
the mixture moist; mix well. Top with the cheese; sprinkle with the pepper. Serve immediately
with a crisp mixed baby green salad tossed in olive oil and balsamic vinegar and some
hard, crusty Italian bread. Biscotti and coffee make a great dessert.

Yield: 4 servings

Cynthia C. Flannery, Jr.

Meats, Poultry, and Seafood
Hobo Dinner

To celebrate the end of a good summer when all the produce was ripe, my family would join friends with this easy-to-cook party recipe. We would serve sliced fresh tomatoes and cucumbers, fresh radishes and corn on the cob to our guests.

7 pounds small potatoes, rinsed
7 pounds mixed bratwurst, Polish sausage and Italian sausage
5 pounds (3-inch) onions, peeled
2 packages fresh carrots, rinsed
2 packages fresh celery, rinsed
1 cup water

Layer the potatoes, sausages, onions, carrots and celery in a foil-lined 5-gallon popcorn can. Add the water. Make a hole in the lid of the can with a small nail. Place the lid on the can and place on the grill. Cook, covered, for 30 to 45 minutes or until steam escapes from the hole. Cook for 1 hour longer.
Yield: 12 to 18 servings

Linn Fallon

Tiny Meatball and Sausage Medley

My grandmother's family migrated to the U.S. in the early 1900s and brought with them many lovely recipes. My grandmother was a gourmet cook and was hired by the Monroe family (of Monroe calculators) as their family chef. She often made this meal on special occasions for my family and handed down the recipe to my mother, Gloria Hunter, who has shared it with me.

1 pound mixed ground veal, beef and pork
3 eggs
2 slices day-old bread, finely chopped
1/2 teaspoon salt   1/2 teaspoon pepper
1/4 cup grated Parmesan cheese
1 teaspoon finely chopped parsley
2 tablespoons vegetable oil
2 tablespoons butter   1 pound Italian sausage
1/4 cup (about) vegetable oil
1 large onion, chopped
2 green bell peppers, chopped
1 jar button mushrooms   2 (14-ounce) cans tomato sauce
1/8 teaspoon dried basil, or to taste
1/8 teaspoon dried mint, or to taste   1 can tiny peas

Combine the veal mixture, eggs, bread crumbs, salt, pepper, cheese and parsley in a bowl and mix well. Shape into 3/4-inch balls. Fry in 2 tablespoons oil and butter in a skillet. Remove with a slotted spoon. Boil the sausage in water to cover in a saucepan for 10 minutes. Let cool. Cut into 1/2-inch slices. Fry the sausage in the skillet until lightly browned. Remove with a slotted spoon. Heat 1/4 cup oil in a large skillet. Add the onion and green peppers. Sauté over low heat until lightly browned. Add the mushrooms. Cook until lightly browned. Add the meatballs and sausage slices and mix gently. Add the tomato sauce, basil and mint and mix gently. Season with additional salt and pepper. Add the peas. Cook until heated through. Serve over hot rice as a main dish or as an accompaniment to pasta.

Yield: 6 servings

Susan Hunter Lyon

Braised Lamb Shanks

6 lamb shanks
1 1/2 teaspoons salt
1/4 teaspoon pepper
3 tablespoons butter or vegetable oil
1/4 cup vinegar
1/2 cup water
2 tablespoons sugar
1 tablespoon prepared mustard
1 1/2 teaspoons salt
1/2 teaspoon pepper
1/4 teaspoon cayenne
1 thick lemon slice
1 cup thinly sliced onion
1/4 cup butter or margarine
1/2 cup catsup
2 tablespoons Worcestershire sauce

Season the lamb with 1 1/2 teaspoons salt and 1/4 teaspoon pepper. Melt 3 tablespoons butter in a Dutch oven. Add the lamb. Simmer until evenly browned. Bring the vinegar, water, sugar, mustard, 1 1/2 teaspoons salt, 1/2 teaspoon pepper, cayenne, lemon, onion, 1/4 cup butter, catsup and Worcestershire sauce to a boil in a saucepan. Simmer for 10 minutes. Pour over the lamb. Simmer, covered, for 2 hours or until the lamb is tender, basting frequently. May be baked at 300 degrees for 2 hours instead of simmering on the stove. I usually double the sauce recipe; after the lamb is done, I strain the fat off the top so I have a fat-free gravy to serve. I also strain off the lemons, but add the onion back for flavor.

Yield: 4 to 6 servings

Mrs. Philip D. Block III

The Bishop's Veal Chops

This veal was served to my husband and me by Bishop John K. Keating of Virginia. While studying at home, he decided he wanted to learn how to cook his favorite Italian dishes. It is a treat to be invited for dinner at his home in Arlington.

1 cup flour
Thyme to taste
Pepper to taste
4 (1-inch) veal chops
1 (16-ounce) package vermicelli
2 tablespoons olive oil
1 package fresh sage leaves
1 cup white wine
1 cup vermouth
$1/4$ cup butter
Freshly grated Parmesan cheese to taste

Mix the flour, thyme and pepper in a shallow dish. Dredge the veal in the flour mixture. Cook the pasta using the package directions. Heat the olive oil in a large skillet. Add the chops and sage. Cook until chops are browned, turning once. Remove and keep warm. Deglaze the skillet with the wine. Return the chops and sage to the skillet. Cook over low to medium heat for 10 minutes. Turn the chops. Cook, covered, for 10 minutes longer. Heat the vermouth and butter in a saucepan. Drain the pasta and arrange on plates. Pour the sauce over the pasta. Sprinkle with the cheese.

Yield: 4 servings

Mrs. Thomas C. Clark

Osso Buco

3 veal shanks
1 to 2 tablespoons olive oil
1/2 cup flour
Salt and pepper to taste
1 cup white wine
3/4 cup chicken broth
2 1/2 cups chopped onions
3 large cloves of garlic, chopped
1/4 cup butter   1/2 cup chopped celery
1 1/4 cups chopped carrots
2 cups chopped fresh tomatoes
2 bay leaves   1/2 teaspoon thyme
1 tablespoon chopped fresh parsley
1 3/4 cups chicken broth
Grated peel of 1 lemon
3 tablespoons minced parsley
2 cloves of garlic, minced

Have the butcher cut the veal shanks crossgrain into 2-inch slices and tie with
string to keep the veal on the bone. Rub the veal with a small amount of the olive oil.
Dredge in a mixture of the flour, salt and pepper. Brown the veal in the remaining olive
oil in a large Dutch oven. Remove the veal and drain off the oil. Simmer the wine
and 3/4 cup chicken broth in the Dutch oven until reduced by 1/4 to 1/2. Pour into a bowl.
Sauté the onions and chopped garlic in the butter in the Dutch oven until the onions are
translucent. Add the celery and carrots. Sauté for 6 to 7 minutes or until the
carrots are tender. Add the wine mixture, tomatoes, bay leaves, thyme, 1 tablespoon
parsley and 1 3/4 cups chicken broth. Bring to a boil. Add the veal. Bake, covered,
at 325 degrees for 2 hours and 10 minutes. Bake, uncovered, for 30 minutes longer
or until the veal is tender. Remove the strings. Sprinkle with a mixture of the lemon peel,
3 tablespoons parsley and minced garlic. Serve with brown rice.
Yield: 6 servings

Sandra K. Crown

Chicken Curry

This is an adaptation from a dear Indian friend living in Paris.

4 skinless chicken breasts
3 tablespoons vegetable oil   2 medium onions, chopped
2 cloves of garlic, crushed
5 teaspoons curry powder, or to taste
1 small piece fresh gingerroot
1 teaspoon ground coriander   1 teaspoon ground cumin
1 teaspoon ground turmeric
1 teaspoon chili powder
1 to 2 tablespoons ground red chile pepper, or to taste
4 large tomatoes, blanched, peeled, finely chopped
2 potatoes, peeled, chopped
1/2 cup frozen peas   1 carrot, peeled, chopped
Salt to taste   Peanuts   Flaked coconut
1/2 to 1 cup raisins
Chopped fresh tomatoes   Mandarin orange slices
Chutney   Chopped fresh coriander leaves   Pompadoms

Rinse the chicken and pat dry. Chop into pieces. Heat the oil in a 6-quart
Dutch oven. Add the onions. Cook until lightly browned. Add the garlic, chicken and curry
powder. Tie the gingerroot onto the pot handle; let the ginger hang down into
the Dutch oven. (Cooked ginger can resemble chicken and is not pleasant to bite into.)
Cook for 5 minutes or until the chicken turns white, stirring constantly. Stir in the coriander,
cumin, turmeric, chili powder and red chile pepper. Add the finely chopped tomatoes,
potatoes, peas and carrot. Season with the salt. Cover and cook over very low
heat until the potatoes are tender. Top with the peanuts, coconut flakes, raisins, chopped
fresh tomatoes, mandarin orange slices, chutney and chopped fresh coriander leaves.
Serve with pompadoms (found in Indian specialty shops).
Yield: 6 servings

Shelly Szychowski and Mark Botelho

Meats, Poultry, and Seafood
Chicken Enchiladas

*My eighteen-month-old loves this recipe, which I originally received from a chef
at a fish restaurant. It has become a favorite because it pleases everyone.*

10 ounces chicken or chicken tenders
2 tablespoons butter
1/4 cup flour
1 cup sour cream
1 cup whipping cream
1/2 can chicken broth
1 package large flour tortillas
2 packages shredded mixed Monterey Jack and Colby cheese

Rinse the chicken and pat dry. Brown the chicken in a nonstick skillet. Let cool and
cut into chunks. Melt the butter in a saucepan. Add the flour, sour cream, whipping
cream and chicken broth. Cook over low to medium heat until thickened, stirring frequently.
Place the chicken on the tortillas. Add enough of the cheese to cover the chicken. Roll up
tightly, securing with wooden picks if needed. Place in a 10x15-inch glass baking
dish; pour the sauce over the rolls. Top with the remaining cheese. Bake at
350 degrees for 25 minutes. Serve with Spanish rice and a salad. May
substitute low-fat ingredients for any of the higher-fat ones.
Yield: 10 servings

Anne Kelly

Meats, Poultry, and Seafood
Herbwood Chicken

Any combination of herbs can be used in this recipe; just be careful to watch the flavors. This dish will provide you with a hot, fragrant, flavorful entrée every time.

2 cups flour   1 tablespoon seasoned salt
1 teaspoon granulated garlic
1 teaspoon pepper   2 tablespoons olive oil
2 large whole chicken breasts, split
1/4 cup chopped fresh basil
2 tablespoons chopped fresh thyme
1/4 cup chopped fresh parsley   2 cloves of garlic, chopped
1/2 teaspoon salt   1/2 teaspoon pepper
Frozen puff pastry, thawed   4 (3- to 4-ounce) slices Brie cheese
1 egg   1 tablespoon cold water

Mix the flour, seasoned salt, granulated garlic and 1 teaspoon pepper in a shallow dish. Heat the olive oil in a 9-inch sauté pan over medium heat. Rinse the chicken in cold water and pat dry. Dredge in the flour mixture, shaking to remove any excess. Place in the sauté pan. Cook for 4 minutes per side or until the chicken is 3/4 cooked through. Remove to a freezerproof plate or tray. Let stand in the freezer for 15 minutes or longer. Mix the basil, thyme, parsley, chopped garlic, salt and 1/2 teaspoon pepper in a bowl. Roll the pastry into four 8-inch squares. Place a slice of cheese in the center of each pastry square. Rub the chicken with some of the herb mixture. Place 1 teaspoon of the herb mixture over the cheese. Top with a piece of chicken. Fold the corners of the pastry to cover the chicken. Beat the egg and water in a small bowl. Brush the pastry with a small amount of the egg wash to seal. Trim away any excess pastry. Turn the chicken puffs and brush with the remaining egg wash. Place on a greased baking sheet. Bake at 400 degrees for 30 minutes. May cut any excess pastry with a cookie cutter and decorate the tops of puffs before baking.

Yield: 4 servings

David DaBoll

Meats, Poultry, and Seafood

Chicken Italian

Kids love this, but it's good enough for guests. It can be made in quantity, and it keeps and reheats well. It also makes a great cold sandwich.

4 boneless skinless chicken breasts, cut into halves
6 tablespoons butter
3 tablespoons Dijon mustard
1 tablespoon white wine or vermouth
1 cup seasoned bread crumbs
1/2 cup grated Parmesan cheese
1 teaspoon Italian herb blend
1/2 teaspoon salt
1 teaspoon pepper

Rinse the chicken and pat dry. Melt the butter in a saucepan. Whisk in the Dijon mustard and wine. Mix the bread crumbs, cheese, herb blend, salt and pepper in a bowl. Dip 1 piece of the chicken into the butter mixture, shaking to remove any excess. Coat with the crumb mixture. Roll lengthwise and place seam side down in an 8x11-inch glass baking dish. Repeat with the remaining chicken. Drizzle with any remaining butter mixture. Bake at 375 degrees for 40 minutes or until the chicken is cooked through.
Yield: 4 servings

Anne O'Laughlin Scott

Savory Stuffed Teriyaki Chicken Breasts

An easy but most delicious entrée.

3/4 cup butter, softened
2/3 cup minced green onions
1 1/2 teaspoons crumbled thyme
1 teaspoon grated lemon peel
12 boneless chicken breast halves
2/3 cup Kikkoman Teriyaki Baste and Glaze

Mix the butter, green onions, thyme and lemon peel in a bowl. Rinse the
chicken and pat dry. Insert 1 rounded tablespoon of the butter mixture
under the skin of each piece of chicken, being careful not to detach the skin.
Press gently to spread the mixture evenly over the chicken. Pour the Teriyaki Baste
and Glaze into a large shallow baking pan. Add the chicken, turning to
coat well. Arrange the chicken skin side up in a single layer in the pan.
Bake at 350 degrees for 30 minutes or until the chicken
is tender and cooked through.
Yield: 10 to 12 servings

Renée S. Crown

Teriyaki Chicken Legs

My three kids love this so much that they fight for the leftovers to bring for lunch the next day! Better yet, they want it for breakfast as well.

1/3 cup fresh lemon juice
1/4 cup catsup
1/4 cup light soy sauce
1/4 cup vegetable oil
2 teaspoons sesame oil
3 tablespoons brown sugar
1 clove of fresh garlic, crushed
1/4 teaspoon freshly ground pepper
1 to 2 teaspoons finely chopped fresh ginger (optional)
14 chicken legs, or 3 pounds

Combine the first 9 ingredients in a 2-cup measure and mix well. Rinse the chicken and pat dry. Place in a sealable 1-gallon freezer bag. Add the marinade and seal. Turn the bag several times to coat the chicken. Marinate in the refrigerator for 8 to 10 hours. Arrange the chicken in a shallow 9x13-inch baking pan. Pour the marinade over the chicken. Bake at 375 degrees for 1 hour and 10 minutes, turning after 35 minutes. Serve with plain rice and steamed vegetables.

Yield: 7 to 14 servings

Marianna Y. Wagner

Le Guajolote por Gringos

I was tired of eating leftover turkey, and I wanted something fancy.

Leftover sliced turkey
Sliced turkey ham
Asparagus
Shredded or sliced mozzarella cheese
1 (10-ounce) can cream of asparagus soup
$1/2$ soup can water
2 tablespoons wine (optional)

Layer the turkey, ham, asparagus and cheese in an 8x12-inch baking dish.
Mix the soup, water and wine in a bowl. Pour over the layers. Bake at 350 degrees
for 20 minutes. Garnish with parsley flakes or rosemary.
Yield: 6 to 8 servings

Jerry Kasdan

Slim Meat Loaf

This variation of meat loaf is a very tasty comfort food.

1 to 1½ pounds ground turkey breast
1 large onion, chopped
1 clove of garlic, minced
1 rib celery, chopped
1 (10-ounce) package frozen spinach, thawed, drained
½ red bell pepper, chopped
½ green bell pepper, chopped
¾ to 1 cup 2% milk
1 egg white
½ cup bread crumbs
1 teaspoon Italian herbs
Salt and pepper to taste
Catsup or mustard to taste

Combine the ground turkey, onion, garlic, celery, spinach and bell peppers in a large bowl and mix well. Add the milk, egg white and bread crumbs and mix well. Season with the herbs, salt and pepper. Pour into a loaf pan. Spread the catsup in a decorative pattern over the top. Bake at 350 degrees for 1 hour. Cut into slices. Serve with mashed potatoes.
Yield: 8 to 12 servings

Leigh S. Buettner

Fish Florentine

2 fish fillets
1 (10-ounce) package frozen spinach soufflé, thawed
1/3 cup cracker crumbs   3 tablespoons grated Parmesan cheese

Place the fish in a greased 7x12-inch baking dish. Cover with the spinach. Sprinkle with the cracker crumbs and Parmesan cheese. Bake at 400 degrees until the fish flakes easily.

Yield: 2 servings

Suzanne S. Dixon

Salmon à la Shedd

This is the favorite fish recipe of the collecting crew on the Shedd Aquarium's collecting boat, the R. V. Coral Reef II. Guaranteed to make your guests say, "Wow—best fish we've ever tasted."

1 cup butter   1 cup fresh lemon juice
1/2 cup dry vermouth   2 teaspoons celery salt
1 teaspoon celery seeds   1/4 teaspoon dillseeds
1/4 teaspoon caraway seeds   1/4 teaspoon onion salt
4 pounds salmon fillets   8 to 10 bay leaves   1/4 cup capers, drained

Melt the butter in a saucepan over low heat. Add the lemon juice, vermouth, celery salt, celery seeds, dillseeds, caraway seeds and onion salt and mix well. Arrange the salmon in two 9x12-inch glass baking dishes sprayed with nonstick cooking spray. Pour the sauce over the salmon. Sprinkle with additional seasonings if desired. Place 1 bay leaf and 6 to 8 capers on each fillet. Bake at 350 degrees for 10 to 15 minutes or until the salmon becomes opaque and flakes easily, basting frequently with the sauce; do not overcook.

Yield: 8 servings

Pat and Bill Braker

Willis Spicy Grilled Salmon Steaks

1 1/2 teaspoons freshly ground black pepper
1/2 teaspoon paprika
1/4 teaspoon cayenne
1 teaspoon minced garlic
1 tablespoon minced onion
1/2 teaspoon crumbled dried thyme
1/4 teaspoon Herbarmare salt
1 tablespoon pressed olive oil
2 (1-pound) salmon steaks, 1-inch thick
1 tablespoon soy margarine
1/2 teaspoon dried basil
1/2 teaspoon dried mint

Combine the black pepper, paprika, cayenne, garlic, onion, thyme, salt
and olive oil in a bowl and mix until a stiff paste forms. Pat the paste onto both sides
of the steaks. Heat an oiled ridged grill pan over medium-high heat until it is
smoking. Add the salmon. Sauté for 3 to 4 minutes per side or until cooked through.
Combine the margarine, basil and mint in a small skillet. Cook over moderate
heat until dark brown, swirling the skillet frequently. Remove the salmon to
heated plates. Pour the margarine sauce over the salmon.
Yield: 2 servings

Jorie Butler Kent

Tuna Niçoise with Mustard Anchovy Vinaigrette

This recipe is an all-time favorite. Although the list looks long, the recipe is really not difficult. It is easy enough to make for a weekday dinner, but also special enough to serve company. It's essential to use good, ripe, flavorful tomatoes.

1 1/2 pounds small new potatoes, cut into 3/4-inch pieces
Salt to taste
Mustard Anchovy Vinaigrette (see page 135)
2 fresh tomatoes, cut into 1/2-inch pieces
1 tablespoon olive oil
1 pound green beans, trimmed, cut into 1-inch pieces
4 (5-ounce) fresh tuna steaks, 1/2-inch thick
1/2 teaspoon salt
1 teaspoon freshly ground pepper
1 tablespoon olive oil
1/4 cup Niçoise olives

Place the potatoes in salted water to cover in a saucepan. Bring to a boil over high heat. Boil for 10 minutes or until tender. Drain and place in an ovenproof bowl. Toss with 3 tablespoons of the vinaigrette. Keep warm in an oven set at a low heat setting. Stir 1 tablespoon of the vinaigrette into the tomatoes. Set aside and keep warm. Heat a large cast-iron skillet over medium-high heat until hot but not smoking. Add 1 tablespoon olive oil. Add the green beans. Stir-fry for 5 minutes or until lightly browned and tender-crisp. Remove from the heat; remove the beans to a bowl. Toss with 1 tablespoon of the vinaigrette. Set aside and keep warm. Season the tuna with the salt and pepper. Return the skillet to medium-high heat. Add 1 tablespoon olive oil. Add the tuna. Cook for 2 to 3 minutes per side or until seared on the outside and medium-rare on the inside. Remove to warm shallow bowls. Distribute the vegetables neatly around the tuna. Top with the olives. Drizzle with the remaining vinaigrette. Serve immediately.

Tuna Niçoise with Mustard Anchovy Vinaigrette

(continued)

Mustard Anchovy Vinaigrette

1 tablespoon anchovy paste
1 medium clove of garlic, minced
2 teaspoons grainy mustard
3 tablespoons balsamic vinegar
$1/4$ cup olive oil
2 teaspoons capers, rinsed
$1/4$ teaspoon salt
$1/4$ teaspoon freshly ground pepper

Whisk the anchovy paste, garlic, mustard and vinegar in a medium bowl. Add the
olive oil gradually, whisking until emulsified. Stir in the capers, salt and pepper.

Yield: 4 servings

Jill and Mike Wallock

Seafood Risotto

 1/2 red onion, chopped
2 cloves of garlic, chopped
2 tablespoons butter
3 tablespoons olive oil
8 ounces large shrimp, peeled
8 ounces sea scallops
1 cup rice
 1/2 cup white wine
2 to 3 cups fish stock
2 tablespoons white wine
5 to 6 fresh basil leaves, chopped
 1/2 cup half-and-half
 1/2 cup grated Parmesan or Romano cheese

Sauté the onion and garlic in the butter and olive oil in a large sauté pan
or skillet until the onion is translucent and the garlic is yellow. Add the shrimp. Cook until
almost done. Remove with a slotted spoon. Add the scallops to the sauté pan.
Cook until almost done. Remove with a slotted spoon. Add the rice to the cooking liquid in
the pan. Cook over medium heat for 2 to 3 minutes, stirring constantly.
Add 1/2 cup wine. Cook until the wine has evaporated. Add a small amount of the
fish stock at a time, stirring constantly after each addition until completely absorbed; this
process will take about 25 minutes. Do not add additional fish stock after the rice
is al dente or done to taste. Add 2 tablespoons wine. Cook until the wine has evaporated.
Add the basil, half-and-half, cheese, shrimp and scallops and mix well. Cook for 2 to 3
minutes or until heated through. Top with additional Parmesan cheese.
Yield: 2 to 3 servings

Anne Ryan

Baked Stuffed Shrimp

1 to 1 1/2 pounds fresh jumbo shrimp
1 large can evaporated milk
3/4 cup Italian bread crumbs
2 sleeves butter crackers, crushed
8 ounces fresh sea scallops
Salt and pepper to taste
1/4 cup butter or margarine
1/4 cup melted butter or margarine

Peel and devein the shrimp, leaving the last section of the shell and
tail intact for holding the shrimp. Cut a small Y into the end of the shrimp. Mix the
evaporated milk, bread crumbs, cracker crumbs, scallops, salt and pepper
in a large bowl. Melt 1/4 cup butter in a 12x12-inch baking pan. Arrange the
shrimp tail side up around the edges of the pan. Fill the center with the
stuffing. Pour 1/4 cup butter over the top. Bake at 350 degrees for
30 minutes or until the shrimp turn pink; do not overcook.
Yield: 4 to 6 servings

Dave Durette

Shrimp in Won Ton Shells

12 won ton wrappers
12 medium shrimp
4 ounces fresh angel hair pasta
6 tablespoons soy sauce
2 tablespoons rice vinegar
3 tablespoons olive oil
1 small onion, chopped
1 small shallot, chopped
1 clove of garlic, minced
1 small green bell pepper, chopped
1 small red bell pepper, chopped
1 can water chestnuts, thinly sliced
2 tablespoons hot Chinese mustard
$1/2$ lime
Chopped parsley to taste

Press the won ton wrappers into oiled muffin cups. Bake at 350 degrees
for 12 minutes or until browned. Boil the shrimp in water to cover in a saucepan. Peel,
devein and chop the shrimp; set aside. Boil the pasta in water to cover in a saucepan for
1 to 2 minutes or until al dente; drain and set aside. Combine the soy sauce, vinegar and
olive oil in a skillet over medium heat. Add the onion, shallot and garlic. Sauté for 1 minute.
Add the bell peppers and water chestnuts. Sauté for 2 minutes. Add the mustard. Sauté
for 1 minute. Add the shrimp. Sauté for 3 minutes. Pour into a bowl. Squeeze the lime juice
over the top. Chill, covered, for 2 hours, stirring occasionally. Place a small amount of pasta
in each won ton shell. Top with the shrimp mixture. Sprinkle with parsley.

Yield: 12 servings

Mrs. Robert D. Krebs

Vegetables
and sides

Vegetables and Sides
The Mysterious Artichoke

6 medium artichokes   Lemon juice
1 cup bread crumbs   1 cup grated Parmesan cheese
Salt and pepper to taste
1 clove of garlic, minced (optional)
1/4 cup olive oil

Hold the artichokes by the stems and plunge up and down quickly in a
deep bowl of water. Cut off the stems with scissors. Trim the top leaves 1/4 inch. Snap
off the bottom row of leaves by bending them back from the core. Dip the trimmed
base in a small amount of lemon juice to prevent discoloration. Mix the bread crumbs,
cheese, salt, pepper and garlic in a bowl. Spread the artichoke leaves apart and stuff with
the cheese mixture. Drizzle with the olive oil. Arrange the artichokes to fit snugly
in a saucepan or steamer. Add enough water to reach the middle of the artichokes.
Steam until the artichokes are tender and a leaf pulls out easily.
Yield: 6 to 8 servings

Andria Christy

Vegetables and Sides
Grandma Blazek's World-Famous Baked Beans

2 (16-ounce) cans baked beans
6 slices bacon, chopped   1 teaspoon dry mustard
3/4 cup packed dark brown sugar
1/2 cup catsup

Combine the beans, bacon, dry mustard, brown sugar and catsup in a bean pot
or baking dish and mix well. Bake at 325 degrees for 2 1/2 hours, stirring occasionally.
Yield: 8 to 12 servings

Vicky Stumpf

The Aquarium uses its research vessel, the R V Coral Reef II,
for collecting animals and for conservation projects.

141

Vegetables and Sides
Creole Red Beans and Rice

This dish is traditionally served on Monday nights in New Orleans households, presumably after a weekend of richer fare and to give the cook a night off.

1 pound dried red beans or kidney beans
9 to 11 cups water
2 teaspoons garlic salt
1/4 teaspoon Tabasco sauce
1 pound cubed ham and/or hot smoked andouille or boudin
2 cups chopped onions
1 cup chopped celery
2 cloves of garlic, minced
3/4 cup chopped green bell pepper
3 tablespoons vegetable oil
2 bay leaves
1/4 teaspoon freshly ground pepper
1/2 teaspoon cumin
1/4 cup chopped parsley
8 to 12 servings steamed white rice

Rinse and sort the beans. Combine with the water, garlic salt, Tabasco sauce and ham in a large, heavy pot. Bring to a boil; reduce the heat to low. Sauté the onions, celery, garlic and green pepper in the oil in a skillet. Add the onion mixture and bay leaves to the beans. Simmer, covered, over low heat for 1 hour or until the beans begin to soften, stirring occasionally and adding additional water if needed. Add the pepper and cumin. Simmer for 1 to 1 1/2 hours or until the beans are soft and creamy, stirring occasionally and adding additional water if needed. Adjust the seasonings. Let stand for several minutes. Remove the bay leaves and stir in the parsley. Serve over the rice. Garnish with Creole or Dijon mustard. May soak the beans overnight to reduce cooking time. For a creamier texture, mash some of the beans against the side of the pot and stir before serving. Best if prepared 1 day ahead. Freezes well.
Yield: 8 to 12 servings

James Dart

Vegetables and Sides
Broccoli Casserole

3 (10-ounce) packages frozen chopped broccoli
12 ounces Velveeta cheese, cubed
$^1/_2$ cup melted butter or margarine
2 sleeves butter crackers, finely crushed

Cook the broccoli using the package directions; drain well. Add the cheese
and mix well. Spoon into a 9x13-inch baking dish. Top with a mixture
of the butter and cracker crumbs. Bake at 350 degrees for 45 minutes. May
substitute mixed broccoli and cauliflower for the broccoli.
Yield: 8 to 12 servings

Michelle Zaversnik

Vegetables and Sides
Cabbage Casserole

$1^1/_2$ pounds ground beef
Minced fresh garlic, garlic salt or garlic powder to taste
3 (10-ounce) cans tomato soup
1 large head cabbage, chopped
8 ounces Colby cheese or Cheddar cheese, cubed

Brown the ground beef with the garlic in a skillet; drain well. Layer the soup,
cabbage, cheese and ground beef in a 4- to 5-quart baking dish. Bake, covered, at 375
degrees for $1^1/_4$ hours or until the cabbage is tender, stirring every 15 minutes.
Yield: 8 to 12 servings

Ronald R. Klain

Baked Corn and Tomatoes

3 cups fresh corn kernels
6 ripe tomatoes, thickly sliced
2 tablespoons finely chopped onion
2 tablespoons butter, cut into pieces
1/4 teaspoon salt, or to taste
1/4 teaspoon pepper, or to taste
1/4 teaspoon sugar, or to taste
1 cup fresh bread crumbs
3 slices bacon, diced

Layer half the corn, tomatoes, onion and butter in a buttered casserole
or baking dish. Sprinkle with half the salt, pepper and sugar. Repeat
the layers and the seasonings. Top with the bread crumbs and bacon.
Bake at 375 degrees for 45 minutes.
Yield: 6 to 8 servings

Suzanne Dixon

Tomatoes Stuffed with Eggplant Spread

This recipe was served to us as a spread for French bread in a lovely restaurant near Long Beach. The waiter was able to give us a list of ingredients but that's all. I think I've duplicated it about right. We like it.

1¼ to 1½ pounds eggplant, peeled, finely chopped
4 to 5 cloves of garlic, finely chopped
½ can (or more) anchovies
1 cup chopped parsley
1 (14-ounce) can artichoke hearts
1 teaspoon pepper
1¼ cups (about) mayonnaise
Plum tomatoes

Combine the eggplant, garlic, anchovies, ¼ cup of the parsley and artichoke hearts in a bowl and mix well. Add the pepper and mayonnaise and mix well. Cut the tomatoes into halves horizontally. Slice the bottom from each tomato half so each will stand upright. Scoop out the seeds and pulp; save for another use or discard. Spoon in the eggplant mixture. Top with the remaining parsley. May use cherry tomatoes and just cut off the top, scoop out pulp and fill with eggplant spread. (May make a spread from the tomato pulp by mixing with sour cream, cream cheese, salsa, Tabasco sauce and anchovies to taste.)
Yield: 8 to 10 servings

Nan Graves

Vegetables and Sides
Garden Mélange

*This recipe was developed by my family in the 1970s
to use all of our garden-fresh produce.*

1 pound summer squash and/or zucchini, sliced
1 medium onion, sliced
1 green bell pepper, chopped
1/2 eggplant, peeled, chopped
1/4 to 1/2 cup butter or margarine
Salt and pepper to taste
4 tomatoes, sliced
1/2 cup bread crumbs (optional)
1 to 1 1/2 cups shredded Cheddar cheese and/or Monterey Jack cheese

Sauté the squash, onion, green pepper and eggplant separately in the
butter in a skillet until lightly browned. Mix the squash, onion, green pepper
and eggplant in a bowl. Season with the salt and pepper. Spoon
into a greased 9x13-inch or 3-quart baking dish. Arrange the tomato
slices over the top. Top with the bread crumbs and cheese. Dot with
additional butter. Bake at 350 degrees for 20 to 25 minutes
or until the vegetables are tender.
Yield: 8 servings

Laris Gross

Vegetables and Sides
Jansson's Temptation

*A dish from Swedish immigrants to bring memories of the
Old Country and tears to one's eyes.*

1 can Swedish anchovy fillets, or 18 fillets
1 cup sliced onions
2 tablespoons butter
4 cups potatoes, cut into thin strips
3 tablespoons plus 1 teaspoon butter
1 cup light cream

Drain the anchovies, reserving 1 tablespoon of the liquid. Sauté the onions
in 2 tablespoons butter in a skillet. Layer half the potatoes, the onions, anchovies and
remaining potatoes in a buttered 1¹/₂-quart baking dish. Sprinkle with the
reserved liquid. Dot with the remaining butter. Pour the cream over the top. Bake,
covered with foil, at 400 degrees for 30 minutes. Bake, uncovered, for 20 to
30 minutes longer or until the potatoes are golden brown.
Yield: 4 servings

Kristine Westerberg

Vegetables and Sides

Patrician Potatoes

8 to 10 baking potatoes, peeled
1 cup sour cream
8 ounces cream cheese, softened
2 teaspoons salt
Minced fresh garlic to taste
Chopped dried chives to taste
Melted butter to taste
Paprika to taste

Cook the potatoes in water to cover until tender; drain well. Beat the sour
cream and cream cheese in a mixer bowl until fluffy. Add the hot potatoes gradually,
beating after each addition. Stir in the salt, garlic and chives. Spoon into
a 2-quart casserole. Brush with the butter and sprinkle with the paprika.
Bake at 350 degrees for 30 minutes. May be frozen before baking.
Yield: 8 to 10 servings

Mrs. Stephen Byron Smith

Vegetables and Sides
Sinful Potatoes

8 ounces bacon
1 pound Velveeta cheese, cubed
2 cups mayonnaise
1 (2-pound) package frozen hash brown potatoes, partially thawed

Cook the bacon in a large skillet until crisp and browned. Drain on paper towels and crumble. Melt the cheese in a heavy saucepan, stirring constantly. Combine the cheese, mayonnaise and potatoes in a large bowl and mix well. Spoon into a large shallow baking dish. Top with the bacon. Bake at 350 degrees for 35 to 40 minutes or until bubbly and golden brown. May be refrigerated or frozen before baking; increase baking time to 1 hour if frozen. Recipe may be halved or doubled.
Yield: 24 servings

Alice W. Stockton

Vegetables and Sides
Mexican Rice

This is the rice recipe I grew up with. My grandmother,
mother and aunts use this recipe.

3/4 cup rice
1 tablespoon vegetable oil
2 cups water
1/2 cup tomato sauce
3/8 teaspoon cumin
Salt to taste
1 small piece of onion
1 small piece of garlic

Sauté the rice in the oil in a 2-quart saucepan. Add the water, tomato sauce,
cumin and salt. Thread the onion and garlic on a toothpick and add to the rice mixture.
Bring to a boil, stirring constantly. Simmer until the water has evaporated.
Remove and discard the onion and garlic.
Yield: 4 servings

Ruth Parciak

Vegetables and Sides

Wild Rice with Almonds and Mushrooms

$^1/_4$ cup butter
1 package wild rice with seasonings
$^1/_2$ cup slivered almonds
2 tablespoons chopped green onions
1 (8-ounce) can sliced mushrooms, drained, or 8 ounces sliced fresh mushrooms
3 cups chicken broth, heated

Melt the butter in a skillet. Add the rice and seasonings, almonds, green
onions and mushrooms. Cook for 20 minutes. Pour into a 1$^1/_2$-quart casserole.
Pour the chicken broth over the mixture and stir well. Bake, covered,
at 325 degrees for 1$^1/_2$ hours or until the mixture is heated through
and the mushrooms and green onions are tender.
Yield: 4 to 6 servings

Diane Horan

Curried Marinated Tomatoes and Mushrooms

*The wife of the Canadian Consul General gave me this recipe
to use at a dinner I was doing for her. I've used it many times since.*

1 teaspoon curry powder
1 teaspoon sugar
1/2 cup vegetable oil
1/4 cup vinegar
1 clove of garlic, crushed
1 tablespoon finely chopped parsley
Salt and pepper to taste
1 (8-ounce) can sliced mushrooms, drained, or
8 ounces sliced fresh mushrooms
5 large tomatoes, sliced

Combine the curry powder, sugar, oil, vinegar, garlic, parsley, salt and pepper in a large bowl and mix well. Add the mushrooms and tomatoes. Marinate, covered, in the refrigerator until thoroughly chilled. Remove the mushrooms and tomatoes from the marinade and arrange attractively on a serving plate. Garnish with chopped green onions.
Yield: 8 servings

Nan Graves

Tofu Indonesian Style

This easy recipe is loved by my vegetarian daughter and my carnivorous teenage son.
It's great to make when I haven't thought in advance about dinner.

$^1/_4$ cup peanut butter
$^1/_4$ cup soy sauce
$^1/_4$ cup water
$^1/_2$ teaspoon sesame oil
$^1/_2$ teaspoon grated fresh ginger
1 teaspoon rice vinegar
1 tablespoon brown sugar
2 cloves of garlic, minced or pressed
1 tablespoon sesame seeds
3 green onions, thinly sliced
1 pound regular or firm tofu, drained, cut into $^1/_2$-inch slices
4 servings hot cooked rice

Combine the peanut butter, soy sauce, water, sesame oil, ginger, vinegar and
brown sugar in a small bowl and mix well. Stir in the garlic, sesame seeds and green
onions. Spoon $^1/_4$ of the peanut butter sauce into an 8x8-inch baking dish. Arrange
the tofu in a single layer over the sauce, trimming the tofu to fit if needed;
tuck the trimmings into the corners of the pan. Spoon the remaining sauce over the tofu.
Bake at 375 degrees for 25 minutes or until the tofu is heated through. Arrange
the tofu on warmed plates. Spoon the rice beside the tofu.
Pour the sauce over the tofu and rice. May serve with chutney.
Yield: 4 servings

Irene J. Check

Tomato Tart

1 1/2 pounds canned plum tomatoes
1 carrot, peeled
1 rib celery
1 medium red onion
Leaves of 10 sprigs of flat leaf parsley
5 basil leaves
2 tablespoons olive oil
2 tablespoons butter
1 1/2 cups flour
1/2 cup butter
1 egg yolk
1/2 teaspoon salt
5 tablespoons ice water
3 eggs
1/2 cup grated Parmesan cheese

Combine the undrained tomatoes, carrot, celery, onion, parsley, basil, olive oil and 2 tablespoons butter in a large saucepan. Simmer for 2 hours or until vegetables are very soft, stirring occasionally. Press through a food mill. Measure out 2 cups of the sauce and let cool. Reserve and store the remaining sauce in the freezer for another purpose. Combine the flour, 1/2 cup butter, egg yolk, salt and ice water in a blender or food processor container. Process until the dough forms a ball. Flatten the ball into a disk and wrap in waxed paper. Chill for 1 hour or longer. Roll the dough to a 1/4-inch thickness on a lightly floured surface, turning frequently. Place in a 9- or 10-inch tart pan with a removable bottom. Pierce holes in the dough with a fork. Cover with weighted foil. Bake at 375 degrees for about 45 minutes or just until done but not browned. Remove the foil. Add the eggs and Parmesan cheese to the cooled sauce and mix well. Pour into the prepared crust. Bake at 375 degrees for 20 minutes or until a knife inserted near the center comes out clean.

Yield: 8 to 12 servings

Betsy Schroeder

Vegetables and Sides
Stuffed Zucchini

3 (6-inch) zucchini
4 ounces mushrooms, chopped
1 carrot, grated
2 tablespoons minced onion
3 tablespoons butter or margarine
$1/2$ teaspoon salt
$1/4$ teaspoon pepper
$1/4$ cup water
1 cup shredded Cheddar cheese or American cheese

Cut the zucchini into halves lengthwise. Scoop out the seeds and some
of the pulp, forming shells. Chop the seeds and pulp. Sauté the seeds, pulp, mushrooms,
carrot and onion in the butter in a skillet. Stir in the salt and pepper. Spoon
into the zucchini shells. Place the shells in a shallow 6x10-inch baking dish. Pour the
water around the shells. Bake, covered with foil, at 375 degrees for 30 minutes.
Sprinkle with the cheese. Bake, uncovered, until the cheese is melted.
Yield: 6 servings

Edna E. Giles

Zucchini Casserole

3 cups thinly sliced zucchini
1 cup baking mix
1/2 cup vegetable oil
2 tablespoons chopped parsley
1/2 cup chopped onion
1 teaspoon oregano
1 teaspoon salt
1/2 teaspoon pepper
1 clove of garlic, chopped
1/2 cup grated Parmesan cheese or Romano cheese
4 eggs, slightly beaten

Combine the zucchini, baking mix, oil, parsley, onion, oregano, salt, pepper, garlic, cheese and eggs in a bowl and mix well. Spoon into a 9x13-inch baking pan sprayed with nonstick cooking spray. Bake at 350 degrees for 25 to 30 minutes or until the mixture is heated through and the zucchini is tender. Cut into squares.
Yield: 20 to 24 servings

Ann Rita Lee

DESSERTS

Desserts
Birthday Cookie

1 cup margarine or butter, softened   1/2 cup sugar
1/2 cup packed brown sugar   1 teaspoon baking soda
1 teaspoon salt   1 teaspoon vanilla extract   2 eggs   2 cups flour
1 1/2 cups chocolate chips or miniature "M & M's" Chocolate Candies

Mix the margarine, sugar, brown sugar, baking soda, salt, vanilla and eggs in a bowl.
Stir in the flour and chocolate chips. Press onto a lightly greased 14-inch pizza pan,
sprinkling the dough with additional flour if needed. Bake at 350 degrees for 12 to 15
minutes or until browned. Cool. Decorate as desired. Slice into wedges.
Yield: 15 to 18 servings

Mina Gardner

Desserts
Almond Chocolate Chip Cookies

2 2/3 cups flour   1 teaspoon baking soda
1 teaspoon salt   1 teaspoon baking powder
2/3 cup sugar   1 1/3 cups packed brown sugar
2 eggs   1 teaspoon vanilla extract
1 teaspoon almond extract   1 cup slightly cooled melted butter
2 (10-ounce) packages large semisweet or milk chocolate chips
2 cups chopped almonds

Mix the first four ingredients together. Cream the sugars, eggs, flavorings and butter
in a mixer bowl. Add flour mixture gradually. Stir in the chocolate chips and almonds.
Drop by ice cream scoops onto a nonstick cookie sheet. Bake at 325 degrees for
15 to 18 minutes or until lightly browned; underbake slightly.
Yield: 2 to 3 dozen

Lorna Monroe

Exquisite architectural details are a signature of
the original 1930 Aquarium building.

Dolores' Chocolate Chip Cookies

*Dolores Jurga, my housekeeper and cook, worked for the St. Charles
Public Schools, where she made over 500 cookies every day. I tell
all my friends these cookies are not fattening because they are made with oats.
When someone says, "How well you look," I answer, "That's because I
eat two or three of Dolores' cookies every day."*

2 cups butter or margarine, softened
1 1/2 cups sugar
1 1/8 cups packed brown sugar
1/2 tablespoon baking soda
1/2 tablespoon salt
1/2 tablespoon vanilla extract
3 eggs
4 cups flour
2 cups rolled oats
1 1/2 cups (or more) semisweet chocolate chips
1 cup grated or chopped French, Swiss or Belgian chocolate
1 cup chopped pecans or walnuts

Cream the butter, sugar and brown sugar in a mixer bowl until light and
fluffy. Beat in the baking soda, salt and vanilla. Add the eggs. Stir in the flour and
oats. Fold in the chocolate chips, chocolate and pecans. Drop by spoonfuls onto
a greased cookie sheet. Bake at 350 degrees for 10 to 12 minutes or
until lightly browned. Cool on a wire rack.
Yield: 8 dozen

Dede Freeman

Cure-All Cookies

Discovered in college, these cookies have cured homesickness, writer's block, pre-final nerves, post-test depression, hunger pangs, chocolate cravings and even an occasional hangover.

1 1/2 cups butter, softened   1 1/2 cups packed brown sugar   1 cup sugar
2 eggs   1 teaspoon vanilla extract   1 tablespoon baking soda
1/2 teaspoon salt   4 cups flour   2 cups chocolate chips

Beat the first 5 ingredients in a mixer bowl until creamy. Add the baking soda, salt and flour and mix well. Stir in the chocolate chips. Drop by rounded tablespoonfuls onto an ungreased cookie sheet. Bake at 350 degrees for 10 to 12 minutes or until lightly browned.

Yield: 4 dozen

Tracy Flanagan

Oatmeal Raisin Cookies

1 1/2 cups unbleached flour   1 teaspoon baking soda
1 teaspoon ground cinnamon   1/2 teaspoon salt   1 1/2 cups rolled oats
1 cup butter, softened   3/4 cup sugar   3/4 cup packed brown sugar
1 teaspoon vanilla extract   1 egg   3/4 cup coarsely chopped pecans
3/4 cup dark raisins or mixed dark and golden raisins

Mix the first 5 ingredients together; set aside. Cream the butter, sugar, brown sugar, vanilla and egg in a mixer bowl until light and fluffy. Add the flour mixture gradually, beating well after each addition. Fold in the pecans and raisins. Drop by tablespoonfuls 2 inches apart onto a buttered cookie sheet. Flatten slightly. Bake at 375 degrees for 10 to 12 minutes or until browned and crisp.

Yield: 2 dozen

Leigh S. Buettner

Desserts

Fred's Favorite Sugar Cookies

2 cups unsalted butter or margarine, softened
1 1/2 cups sugar   3 1/2 cups flour   2 teaspoons vanilla extract

Cream the butter in a mixer bowl until light and fluffy. Add the sugar and mix well. Add the flour gradually, beating at low speed after each addition. Beat in the vanilla. Shape into 1-inch balls. Place 12 balls on each ungreased cookie sheet. Flatten with a cookie stamp or a glass dipped in sugar. Bake at 350 degrees for 10 minutes or until lightly browned. Cool on the cookie sheet for 1 minute. Remove to a wire rack to cool completely.

Yield: 6 to 8 dozen

Fred and Sue Parsons

Desserts

Swedish Spritz

My grandmother was given this recipe by an old family friend.
This recipe was hard to part with.

2 1/2 cups (about) flour   1 teaspoon baking powder
1 cup butter, softened   1 cup (scant) sugar
1 egg   1/2 teaspoon almond extract   Vanilla extract to taste

Sift the flour and baking powder together. Cream the butter and sugar in a mixer bowl until light and fluffy. Add the egg and flavorings and beat well. Add the flour mixture gradually, beating well after each addition until a smooth dough forms. Press through a cookie press fitted with a star-shaped tip onto a nonstick cookie sheet into an "S" shape. Bake at 400 degrees for 8 to 10 minutes or until lightly browned.

Yield: 2 to 3 dozen

Mrs. William Hokin

Desserts

Tahini Treasure Cookies

1 cup raisins   1 cup tahini   ¼ cup honey   ¾ cup sunflower seeds
2¼ cups rolled oats   ½ cup organic barley malt

Soak the raisins in hot water to cover in a bowl until plump; drain. Combine the tahini and honey in a saucepan. Cook over low heat until heated through. Add the sunflower seeds, oats, malt and raisins and mix well. Drop by teaspoonfuls onto a nonstick cookie sheet. Press with a wet fork. Bake at 325 degrees for 15 to 20 minutes or until lightly browned.

Yield: 1 dozen

Jorie Butler Kent

Desserts

Irving Bars

*Irving Bars were adapted from other recipes by my mom, Lois.
She made them for my dad because he liked to get up at 2:00 a.m. and be a gobbling cookie monster. She thought these would at least be a little healthy.*

⅔ cup butter, softened   1 cup packed brown sugar
½ cup corn syrup   1 tablespoon vanilla extract
4 cups quick-cooking oats   1 cup milk chocolate chips
⅔ cup chunky peanut butter   1 cup crisp rice cereal

Cream the butter and brown sugar in a mixer bowl until light and fluffy. Add the corn syrup, vanilla and oats, stirring by hand until well mixed. Spread evenly in a nonstick 9x13-inch baking pan. Bake at 350 degrees for 20 minutes. Let cool for 15 minutes. Combine the chocolate chips and peanut butter in a microwave-safe bowl. Microwave until melted, stirring at 1-minute intervals. Stir in the cereal quickly. Spread over the cooled layer. Let stand until set. Cut into bars with a sharp knife. Store, covered, at room temperature.

Yield: 2 dozen

Cynthia Hart

Desserts

Italian Krustols

This recipe is from my spirited Italian grandmother.

6 eggs
2 tablespoons baking powder
1 teaspoon salt
4 cups (about) flour   Vegetable oil for frying
Honey to taste   Confectioners' sugar to taste

Mix the eggs, baking powder and salt in a bowl. Add enough of the flour to form a pie-like dough. Shape into 3 squares on a lightly floured surface. Cut each square into 1 1/2- to 2x6-inch strips. Cut a small slit in the top left corner of each strip and pull the strip through the slit. Heat the oil to 400 degrees in a skillet. Add the dough pieces. Cook until golden brown, turning once. Place on paper towels. Let stand for 8 to 10 hours. Brush with the honey. Sprinkle with confectioners' sugar.

Yield: 4 dozen

Patricia Valente Witzke

Desserts

Nuttaly Noodaly Clusters

I received this recipe in kindergarten; it's still a favorite in graduate school.

1 cup butterscotch chips   1 cup semisweet chocolate chips
1 (3-ounce) can chow mein noodles   1 cup salted cashews

Melt the butterscotch chips and chocolate chips in a double boiler over hot water. Remove from the heat. Stir in the noodles and cashews. Drop by teaspoonfuls onto a cookie sheet lined with waxed paper. Chill for 1 hour or until set.

Yield: 2 1/2 dozen

Amy Steckel

Desserts
Lemon Squares

*I've made this quick and easy recipe many times, and it always turns out well.
It makes my mom happy when I bring some home to her.*

3/4 cup butter   1 1/2 cups flour   1/3 cup confectioners' sugar
3 eggs   3 tablespoons flour   1 1/2 cups sugar   1/4 cup lemon juice
Confectioners' sugar

Mix the butter, 1 1/2 cups flour and 1/3 cup confectioners' sugar in a large bowl. Press
into an ungreased 9x13-inch baking dish. Bake at 350 degrees for 20 minutes or until
lightly browned. Mix the eggs, 3 tablespoons flour, sugar and lemon juice in a bowl. Pour
over the hot or cooled baked layer. Bake for 20 minutes longer. Cool on a wire
rack. Sprinkle lightly with additional confectioners' sugar.
Yield: 1 1/4 dozen

Paula Resk

Desserts
Toffee Butter Bars

1 cup margarine, softened   1 cup packed brown sugar
1 egg   1 teaspoon vanilla extract
2 cups flour   8 (1.5-ounce) chocolate candy bars
Chopped walnuts or pecans to taste (optional)

Cream the margarine and brown sugar in a mixer bowl until light and fluffy.
Beat in the egg and vanilla. Add the flour gradually, mixing well after each addition.
Spread in a greased 10x15-inch baking pan. Bake at 350 degrees for 15 to
20 minutes or until lightly browned. Arrange the candy bars over the hot layer. Let stand
until melted; spread evenly over the top. Sprinkle with the walnuts.
Yield: 2 dozen

Barbara A. Shedd

Desserts
Turtle Bars

1 (16-ounce) package graham crackers   1 cup margarine
1 cup packed brown sugar   1 1/2 cups chopped walnuts
1 (7-ounce) chocolate candy bar, melted   1 teaspoon vegetable oil

Line a 9x13-inch pan with the graham crackers. Melt the margarine in a saucepan. Add the brown sugar and walnuts. Boil for 3 minutes, stirring constantly. Pour over graham crackers. Spread with a mixture of the chocolate and oil. Cool in the refrigerator. Cut into bars.
Yield: 1 1/4 dozen

Rose M. Swan

Desserts
English Toffee

2 cups lightly salted butter, softened   2 cups sugar
1/2 to 3/4 cup chopped walnuts or pecans
1 1/2 to 2 pounds prepared chocolate or white chocolate coating

Combine the butter and sugar in a heavy saucepan. Cook over medium heat until the mixture reaches 234 to 240 degrees on a candy thermometer, soft-ball stage. Stop stirring and reduce the heat slightly. Cook until the mixture reaches 300 to 310 degrees on a candy thermometer, hard-crack stage. Remove from the heat. Let stand until the mixture almost stops bubbling. Spread the walnuts in a 9x13-inch metal pan. Pour the toffee over the walnuts. Place on a wire rack. Score the toffee into bite-size pieces with a knife as the mixture cools. Cool for 1 hour or longer. Melt the chocolate in a double boiler over simmering water. Remove from the heat. Invert the toffee onto waxed paper. Break along the score lines. Drop the pieces into the coating. Remove with a fork to waxed paper. Chill for 5 minutes.
Yield: 4 pounds

Sharon A. Carpenter

Desserts

Quick Fudge

2 cups chocolate chips   1 (14-ounce) can sweetened condensed milk
1 teaspoon vanilla extract

Melt the chocolate chips in a double boiler over simmering water. Stir in the condensed milk and vanilla. Spread in a well-greased dish. Let stand until cool. Cut into pieces.

Yield: 1 dozen

Lois Smith

Desserts

Marshmallows

2¹/₂ tablespoons unflavored gelatin   ³/₄ cup cold water   2 cups sifted sugar
³/₄ cup hot water   1 cup light corn syrup   1¹/₂ teaspoons vanilla extract
Several drops of food coloring (optional)

Combine the gelatin and cold water in a bowl and mix well. Let stand until thickened. Mix the sifted sugar, hot water and half the corn syrup in a 2-quart saucepan. Bring to a boil, stirring frequently. Cook to 240 degrees on a candy thermometer in cold weather or 242 degrees in warm weather. Do not stir after the mixture begins to boil; wash the sugar crystals from the side of the pan occasionally. Turn off the heat. Add the remaining corn syrup quickly and mix well. Add the gelatin mixture a small amount at a time, mixing until partially dissolved. Pour into a mixer bowl. Beat at low speed for 1 to 2 minutes. Beat at high speed for 10 minutes or until the creme is lukewarm, snow white, heavy and the consistency of whipped cream. Beat in the vanilla and food coloring. Pour into a greased 9x13-inch pan or greased egg molds. Chill for 8 hours or longer. Loosen from the sides of the pan. Place on a lightly floured surface. Cut with a greased knife and roll in the flour until covered. Keeps well for 1 week or for 2 weeks if refrigerated.

Yield: 1 to 1¹/₂ pounds

James Miner

Desserts

Apple Cake with Hot Caramel Sauce

This is an old Amish recipe and is a wonderfully rich, sweet and delicious dessert. It will keep for one week in the refrigerator and freezes well. The caramel sauce may be made one day ahead but may not be frozen.

1/2 cup butter, softened
1 cup sugar
1 egg
1 teaspoon baking soda
1/4 teaspoon salt
1 teaspoon cinnamon
3/4 teaspoon nutmeg
1 cup flour
2 1/2 cups chopped peeled Granny Smith apples
1/2 cup butter
1 cup packed brown sugar
1/2 teaspoon salt
1 teaspoon vanilla extract
1/2 cup evaporated milk

Beat 1/2 cup butter in a mixer bowl until light. Add the sugar and beat until fluffy. Beat in the egg. Stir in the baking soda, 1/4 teaspoon salt, cinnamon and nutmeg. Add the flour, stirring just until blended. Stir in the apples. Pour into an oiled 9-inch round cake pan. Bake at 350 degrees for 30 minutes or until the top springs back when lightly touched. Combine 1/2 cup butter, brown sugar and 1/2 teaspoon salt in a saucepan. Cook until the butter is melted. Bring to a boil, whisking constantly. Remove from the heat. Whisk in the vanilla and evaporated milk. Ladle 2 to 3 tablespoons of the sauce onto each of 8 serving plates. Cut the cake into 8 wedges and place over the sauce. Garnish each serving with a dollop of whipped cream and a sprinkle of nutmeg. Reheat the sauce over hot water if prepared ahead.

Yield: 8 servings

Lisa Reed

Desserts

Avon Antique Apple Cake

I bake this cake every fall after picking apples.

3/4 cup sugar   1 cup flour   1/4 cup butter, softened
1 teaspoon baking powder   1 teaspoon vanilla extract   1 egg
1 to 2 apples, peeled, thinly sliced
2 tablespoons sugar
2 tablespoons butter, softened   1 teaspoon cinnamon
1 egg yolk

Mix 3/4 cup sugar, flour, 1/4 cup butter, baking powder, vanilla and egg in a bowl; the mixture will be dry. Spread in a greased 8-inch round cake pan. Arrange the apple slices in concentric circles over the batter, completely covering the batter. Bake at 350 degrees for 45 minutes. Mix 2 tablespoons sugar, 2 tablespoons butter, cinnamon and egg yolk in a bowl. Spread over the hot cake. Bake for 25 minutes longer.

Yield: 8 servings

Atsuko Shibata

Desserts

Apple Walnut Cake

4 cups coarsely chopped apples   2 cups sugar   1/2 cup vegetable oil
1 cup chopped walnuts   2 eggs, beaten   2 teaspoons vanilla extract
2 cups flour   1 teaspoon salt   2 teaspoons baking soda
2 teaspoons cinnamon

Mix the apples and sugar in a large bowl. Add the oil, walnuts, eggs and vanilla and mix well. Add the remaining ingredients and mix well. Pour into a greased 9x13-inch cake pan. Bake at 350 degrees for 45 to 60 minutes or until a wooden pick inserted near the center comes out clean. Spread with favorite frosting or serve with whipped cream or ice cream.

Yield: 15 servings

Rose M. Swan

Chocolate Cake

2 teaspoons baking soda   2 cups buttermilk
1 ounce unsweetened chocolate   2 cups sugar   2 eggs
3 1/4 cups flour, sifted 3 times   6 tablespoons butter or margarine, softened
1 teaspoon vanilla extract   3 ounces cream cheese, softened
2 tablespoons buttermilk   1/8 teaspoon salt, or to taste
3 ounces chocolate, melted   3 cups confectioners' sugar

Dissolve the baking soda in 2 cups buttermilk. Melt 1 ounce chocolate in a cup
set in a pan of hot water. Combine with the buttermilk mixture, sugar, eggs, sifted flour,
butter and vanilla in a large bowl and mix well. Pour into 2 nonstick 8- or 9-inch cake pans.
Bake at 325 degrees for 30 to 45 minutes or until the layers test done. Combine the cream
cheese, 2 tablespoons buttermilk, salt and 3 ounces chocolate in a mixer bowl. Add the
confectioners' sugar gradually, beating until of a spreading consistency. Frost the cake.

Yield: 12 servings

Joanne Zimmerman

Nutty Birthday Cake

1 cup sugar   1/2 cup butter, softened   3 egg yolks, beaten
2 cups bread flour   2 teaspoons baking powder   1 cup chopped walnuts
3 egg whites, stiffly beaten   1 teaspoon vanilla extract
1 recipe buttercream frosting   Melted bittersweet chocolate to taste

Combine the sugar, butter, egg yolks, bread flour and baking powder in a mixer bowl
and mix well. Stir in the walnuts. Fold in the egg whites and vanilla. Pour into a
greased tube pan. Bake at 350 degrees for 35 minutes. Cool in the pan for several minutes.
Invert onto a serving plate. Spread with the frosting. Drizzle with the chocolate.

Yield: 16 servings

David, Jane and Elena Villa

Desserts

Best-Ever Pineapple Carrot Cake with Cream Cheese Frosting

This carrot cake is excellent with or without the coconut, walnuts or sunflower seeds and with or without frosting. It was clipped from a magazine in 1979 and I modified it to increase fiber and decrease fat. Everyone always loves it.

1 cup all-purpose flour   1 cup whole wheat flour
2 teaspoons baking soda
1 teaspoon baking powder
1 teaspoon salt   2 teaspoons ground cinnamon
1 cup sugar
3/4 cup packed brown sugar
1 cup vegetable oil   2 eggs
1 teaspoon vanilla extract   2 cups shredded carrots
1 cup flaked coconut (optional)
1 cup chopped walnuts or sunflower seeds (optional)
1 (8-ounce) can crushed pineapple, drained
4 ounces low-fat cream cheese, softened
1/4 cup margarine or butter, softened
1 1/2 cups confectioners' sugar   1/2 teaspoon vanilla extract
1 teaspoon milk

Sift the all-purpose flour, whole wheat flour, baking soda, baking powder, salt and cinnamon into a large bowl. Make a well in the center. Add the sugar, brown sugar, oil, eggs and 1 teaspoon vanilla. Beat with a wooden spoon until smooth. Stir in the carrots, coconut, walnuts and pineapple. Pour into a greased and lightly floured 9x13-inch cake pan. Bake at 350 degrees for 45 minutes or until the center springs back when lightly touched. Cool in the pan on a wire rack. Beat the cream cheese and margarine in a mixer bowl until smooth. Beat in the confectioners' sugar and 1/2 teaspoon vanilla. Beat in enough of the milk to make of a spreading consistency. Spread over the cooled cake.

Yield: 15 servings

Alison Paine

Pound Cake

This cake does not use any leavening, only the extensive beating of the eggs. Commercially developed baking powder was first used in 1889; this recipe predates that.

1 cup butter, softened   1²/₃ cups sugar
5 eggs   2 cups cake flour, sifted

Cream the butter in a mixer bowl. Add the sugar, beating constantly until the mixture is light and fluffy and the sugar is dissolved. Add the eggs 1 at a time, beating well after each addition. Add the cake flour gradually, beating well after each addition. Pour into a greased and floured loaf pan. Bake at 350 degrees for 60 to 70 minutes or until a wooden pick inserted near the center comes out clean.
Yield: 12 servings

Lane Ann and Frances Edwards

Spiced Pound Cake

1 cup butter, softened   1¹/₂ teaspoons ground nutmeg   ¹/₂ teaspoon salt
1²/₃ cups sugar   4 eggs   2 cups sifted cake flour   1 egg

Combine the butter, nutmeg and salt in a mixer bowl. Beat for 4 minutes. Blend in the sugar gradually, beating constantly for 2 minutes. Beat in 4 eggs 1 at a time, beating for 15 seconds after each addition. Add the cake flour all at once. Beat for 2 minutes. Blend in the remaining egg, beating for 15 seconds. Pour into a greased and lightly floured 9-inch tube pan. Place in a cold oven. Set the oven temperature to 300 degrees. Bake for 1¹/₂ to 2 hours or until a wooden pick inserted near the center comes out clean. Cool in the pan for 10 minutes. Invert onto a wire rack to cool completely.
Yield: 12 servings

Mrs. Stephen Byron Smith

Desserts
Black Bottom Pie

$1/2$ cup sugar
1 tablespoon cornstarch
2 cups milk
4 egg yolks, beaten
1 teaspoon vanilla extract
1 cup chocolate chips
1 baked (9-inch) pie shell
1 envelope unflavored gelatin
$1/4$ cup cold water
4 egg whites
$1/2$ cup sugar
1 cup whipping cream, whipped

Combine $1/2$ cup sugar and cornstarch in a bowl. Heat the milk in the top of a double boiler until scalded. Stir a small amount of the hot milk into the egg yolks; stir the egg yolks into the hot milk. Add the sugar mixture. Cook over boiling water until the custard coats a spoon, stirring constantly. Stir in the vanilla. Combine 1 cup of the hot custard with the chocolate chips in a bowl, stirring until the chocolate is melted. Pour into the pie shell. Chill thoroughly. Soften the gelatin in the cold water in a small bowl. Add the remaining hot custard, stirring until the gelatin is dissolved. Let stand until cool. Chill, covered, in the refrigerator until slightly thickened. Beat the egg whites in a mixer bowl. Add $1/2$ cup sugar gradually, beating constantly until stiff peaks form. Fold into the custard. Pour over the chocolate layer. Chill until set. Top with the whipped cream. Garnish with chocolate curls.

Yield: 8 servings

Mrs. William N. Sick

Desserts
Lemon Delight Pie

1 1/4 cups fine graham cracker crumbs   1/4 cup sugar
6 tablespoons melted butter or margarine
8 ounces cream cheese, softened   1/3 cup sugar
1 cup sour cream   2 teaspoons vanilla extract
8 ounces whipped topping
1 (3-ounce) package lemon pudding and pie filling mix

Mix the crumbs, 1/4 cup sugar and butter in a bowl. Press firmly into a 9-inch pie plate. Bake at 375 degrees for 6 to 9 minutes or until the edge is browned. Let stand until cool. Beat the cream cheese in a mixer bowl until smooth. Beat in 1/3 cup sugar gradually. Blend in the sour cream and vanilla. Fold in the whipped topping. Spoon into the crust. Chill for 4 hours or until set. Prepare the pie filling using the package directions. Pour over the cream cheese mixture. Chill until set. Garnish with additional whipped topping.

Yield: 8 servings

Arthur F. Jeczala

Desserts
Caribbean Fudge Pies

4 cups semisweet chocolate chips   1/2 cup butter, softened
1 1/2 cups packed brown sugar   6 eggs
1/2 cup flour   2 cups walnut or pecan pieces
2 (9-inch) deep-dish pie shells

Melt the chocolate in a double boiler over simmering water. Cream the butter and brown sugar in a mixer bowl until light and fluffy. Beat in the eggs 1 at a time. Add the flour and 1 cup of the walnuts and mix well. Spoon into the pie shells. Top with the remaining 1 cup walnuts. Bake at 375 degrees for 25 minutes. Let cool. Garnish with whipped cream.

Yield: 16 servings

Linda Wilson

Pecan Pie

I received this recipe from a family in Alabama. It uses half the amount of sugar in most recipes. If you use a deep-dish pie shell, double the recipe.

1 cup mixed chopped and whole pecans   1 unbaked (9-inch) pie shell
1/2 cup sugar   1 cup corn syrup   1/4 cup butter
1/4 teaspoon salt   3 eggs, beaten   1/2 teaspoon vanilla extract

Arrange the pecans in the pie shell. Combine the sugar, corn syrup, butter and salt in a saucepan. Bring to a boil over low heat, stirring frequently. Stir a small amount of the hot mixture into the eggs; stir the eggs into the hot mixture. Cool for several minutes. Stir in the vanilla. Pour over the pecans. Bake at 400 degrees for 10 minutes. Reduce the oven temperature to 375 degrees. Bake for 35 to 40 minutes longer or until a knife inserted near the center comes out clean.

Yield: 8 servings

Mrs. G. Robert Muehlhauser

Strawberry Pie

4 cups whole strawberries
1 baked (9-inch) pie shell   1 cup sugar
2 1/2 tablespoons cornstarch   1 teaspoon vanilla extract

Arrange 2 cups of the strawberries in the pie shell. Combine the remaining strawberries, sugar and cornstarch in a blender container. Process until mixed. Pour into a saucepan. Bring to a boil; reduce heat. Simmer for 15 minutes or until thickened, stirring occasionally. Let cool. Stir in the vanilla. Pour over the whole strawberries. Chill thoroughly. Garnish with whipped cream.

Yield: 8 servings

Louise M. Flannery

Desserts
Mile-High Strawberry Pie

An excellent dessert that can be prepared a day in advance.

2 egg whites   1 cup sugar
1 teaspoon cream of tartar
1 (8-ounce) package frozen strawberries, partially thawed
1 cup whipping cream
1 baked (9-inch) pie shell

Beat the egg whites in a large mixer bowl until soft peaks form. Add the sugar and cream of tartar gradually, beating constantly until stiff peaks form. Beat in the strawberries. Beat for 20 minutes or until the meringue is a "mile high." Beat the whipping cream in a medium mixer bowl until stiff peaks form. Fold into the meringue. Pour into the pie shell. Freeze for 6 to 10 hours.

Yield: 6 to 8 servings

Renée S. Crown

Desserts
Apple Cobbler

6 to 10 apples, thinly sliced
Cinnamon to taste
5 slices white bread, cubed
3/4 cup cooled melted margarine
1 1/2 cups sugar   2 eggs, lightly beaten

Arrange the apples in a 9x13-inch baking pan. Sprinkle with the cinnamon. Top with the bread cubes. Sprinkle with additional cinnamon. Mix the margarine, sugar and eggs in a bowl. Pour over the bread cubes. Bake at 350 degrees for 1 hour. Store in the refrigerator.

Yield: 15 servings

Michelle Zaversnik

Desserts
Apple Crisp

4 cups sliced peeled apples
1 teaspoon cinnamon
1 teaspoon salt
1/4 cup water
3/4 cup flour   1 cup sugar
1/3 cup butter, softened

Arrange the apples in a buttered 6x10-inch glass baking dish. Sprinkle with the
cinnamon, salt and water. Mix the flour and sugar in a bowl. Cut in the
butter until crumbly. Sprinkle over the apples. Bake at 350 degrees for 45 to
50 minutes or until the mixture is heated through and the apples are tender.
May sprinkle with additional cinnamon before baking.
Yield: 8 to 10 servings

Cathy Dismuke

Desserts
Bananas in Rum Sauce

2 large bananas, thinly sliced
Lemon Juice
Dark brown sugar
Dark rum
Whipped cream
Nutmeg

Arrange a single layer of bananas in a shallow dish. Sprinkle with the lemon
juice, brown sugar and rum. Repeat the layers until all the banana slices are used. Chill,
covered, for 2 hours or longer. Top with the whipped cream and sprinkle with the nutmeg.
Yield: 2 servings

Linda Wilson

Banana Split Dessert

This is such a cool and refreshing dessert that it has become a summertime favorite, especially at Fourth of July cookouts.

1 (20-ounce) can crushed pineapple   4 or 5 large bananas, sliced lengthwise
2 cups vanilla wafer crumbs   1/2 cup melted butter
1 (1-pound) package confectioners' sugar   2 eggs   1 cup butter, softened
1 teaspoon vanilla extract   1 cup chopped pecans or walnuts
16 ounces whipped topping

Drain the pineapple, reserving the juice in a bowl. Place the banana slices in the reserved juice to prevent discoloration. Mix the crumbs and melted butter in a bowl. Press into a 9x13-inch pan. Beat the next 4 ingredients in a mixer bowl until creamy. Spread over the crumb mixture. Cover with the drained banana slices. Spread the pineapple over the bananas. Sprinkle with the pecans. Spread with the whipped topping. Chill for 4 to 6 hours.
Yield: 12 to 15 servings

Kelly Galbraith

Cherry Cream Cheesecake

1 1/2 cups graham cracker crumbs   1/4 cup sugar   1/2 cup melted margarine
1/4 cup milk   8 ounces cream cheese, softened   1/2 cup sugar
1/4 cup milk   1 envelope whipped topping mix   1 can cherry or blueberry pie filling

Mix the crumbs, 1/4 cup sugar and margarine in a bowl. Press into a 9x9-inch baking pan. Bake at 350 degrees for 10 minutes. Whip 1/4 cup milk into the cream cheese in a bowl. Mix in 1/2 cup sugar. Whip 1/4 cup milk into the whipped topping mix in a bowl. Fold into the cream cheese mixture. Spread over the cooled crust. Spread with the pie filling. Chill for 8 to 10 hours.
Yield: 9 to 12 servings

Pat Leverick

Desserts
Crème Brûlée

3 cups whipping cream
1 cup half-and-half
1 cup sugar
12 egg yolks, beaten
1/2 cup (about) Demerara sugar or any natural and unrefined sugar

Heat the whipping cream, half-and-half and sugar in a saucepan, stirring until the sugar is dissolved. Stir a small amount of the hot mixture into the egg yolks; stir the egg yolks into the hot mixture. Pour into a shallow casserole or individual ramekins. Place the casserole in a pan of water. Bake at 225 degrees for 2 hours or until set. Remove from the pan of water and let cool. Sprinkle with the Demerara sugar. Broil for 30 seconds or until the sugar dissolves and browns. Chill for 2 hours or longer. May be prepared 1 day ahead.
Yield: 8 to 12 servings

Mrs. Stephen Byron Smith

Desserts
A Delicious Dessert

8 to 10 tablespoons Quaker 100% Natural cereal with raisins
1 quart vanilla ice cream or frozen yogurt
6 to 7 1/2 tablespoons Kahlúa

Place 2 tablespoons of the cereal in each of 4 to 5 dessert plates or bowls. Top each with a scoop of ice cream. Pour 1 1/2 tablespoons Kahlúa over each serving. Serve immediately.
Yield: 4 to 5 servings

Sallie VanArsdale

Desserts

Edible Aquariums

This is great for kids' birthday parties or fun to make on rainy days.

4 (3-ounce) packages berry blue gelatin   2^1/$_2$ cups boiling water
1 package gummy fish or sharks

Dissolve the gelatin in the boiling water. Pour into a 9x13-inch pan. Chill for
3 hours or until firm. Cut into 1x1^1/$_2$-inch pieces. Arrange 11 gelatin pieces and
approximately 8 gummy fish in each of eight 8-ounce clear plastic cups. Serve immediately.
May store any remaining gelatin, covered, in the refrigerator for up to 4 days.
Yield: 8 servings

Amy B. Ihde

Desserts

Heath Bar Cake

12 (1.4-ounce) Heath bars ^{1}/$_2$ cup butter or margarine, softened ^{1}/$_2$ cup sugar
1 cup packed dark brown sugar   2 cups flour, sifted   1 egg
1 teaspoon baking soda   1 teaspoon (or more) vanilla extract
1 cup buttermilk ^{1}/$_8$ teaspoon salt, or to taste

Grind the candy in a food processor. Combine the butter, sugar, brown sugar and sifted
flour in the food processor container. Process until mixed. Combine ^{1}/$_2$ cup of the flour
mixture with the candy in a bowl and mix well. Add the egg, baking soda, vanilla,
buttermilk and salt to the remaining flour mixture. Process until mixed. Pour into a 9x13-inch
baking pan sprayed with nonstick cooking spray. Spread with half the candy mixture. Bake
at 350 degrees for 20 minutes. Spread with the remaining candy mixture. Bake for 10 to
20 minutes longer or until a wooden pick inserted near the center comes out clean.
Yield: 12 to 15 servings

Anna-Marie Brodsky

Desserts

Glazed Rhubarb Pudding

4 cups ¹/₂-inch rhubarb pieces   ²/₃ cup sugar
1 cup flour   2 teaspoons baking powder   ¹/₄ teaspoon salt
¹/₄ cup shredded coconut   ¹/₄ cup butter, softened   ¹/₃ cup sugar
1 teaspoon grated orange peel   ¹/₂ cup milk   ¹/₂ teaspoon vanilla extract
¹/₄ cup sugar   1 tablespoon cornstarch   ¹/₂ cup boiling water

Mix the rhubarb and ²/₃ cup sugar in a bowl. Spoon into a greased shallow
baking dish. Sift the flour, baking powder and salt into a large bowl. Stir in the coconut.
Cream the butter in a mixer bowl until light and fluffy. Add ¹/₃ cup sugar gradually, beating
well after each addition. Stir in the orange peel. Mix the milk and vanilla in a small bowl.
Add the flour mixture and flavored milk alternately to the creamed mixture, beating lightly
after each addition. Drop by spoonfuls over the rhubarb and spread evenly. Sprinkle
with a mixture of ¹/₄ cup sugar and cornstarch. Drizzle with the boiling water. Bake at
375 degrees for 40 minutes or until the rhubarb is tender.

Yield: 6 servings

Mr. and Mrs. T. C. Wright

Desserts

Schaum Tortes

4 egg whites   1 cup sugar
¹/₂ teaspoon cream of tartar   1 teaspoon vanilla extract

Combine the egg whites, sugar and cream of tartar in a mixer bowl. Beat at high
speed for 10 minutes. Stir in the vanilla. Beat at high speed for 15 minutes longer. Pile high
in 6 to 8 greased muffin cups. Place in a cold oven. Turn the oven temperature to
225 degrees. Bake for 45 minutes. Serve with ice cream and raspberries or other fruit.

Yield: 6 to 8 servings

Mr. and Mrs. William L. Harwood

Tiramisù

40 to 48 ladyfingers   12 espresso cups espresso
3 tablespoons rum
3 egg yolks   5 tablespoons sugar
6 ounces cream cheese, softened
3 egg whites, stiffly beaten   6 tablespoons baking cocoa

Soak the ladyfingers in a mixture of the espresso and rum. Beat the egg yolks
and sugar in a mixer bowl until thick and pale yellow. Add the cream cheese, beating until
smooth. Fold the beaten egg whites into the mixture. Layer the ladyfingers and
the cream cheese mixture 1/3 at a time in a shallow glass dish. Dust
with the cocoa. Chill for 6 to 10 hours before serving.
Yield: 6 servings

Michael Delfini

Frozen Zabaglione

1/2 envelope unflavored gelatin   2 tablespoons cold water
8 egg yolks   2/3 cup sugar
1 tablespoon grated lemon peel   1 cup marsala, Cognac or port
3 tablespoons Grand Marnier   2 cups whipping cream, whipped

Dissolve the gelatin in the water in a small bowl. Beat the egg yolks in a double
boiler. Add the sugar, lemon peel and marsala. Cook over simmering water until thickened,
beating constantly. Place the top of the double boiler in a bowl of ice. Stir in the gelatin
mixture and Grand Marnier. Beat until the mixture is cold. Fold in the whipped cream.
Spoon into individual dishes, a mold or an attractive serving bowl.
Freeze for several hours. May serve with fresh raspberries.
Yield: 6 to 8 servings

Betty Hochstadter

Special
Occasions

Special Occasions
Agora Punch

4 quarts cranberry juice
3 quarts water
3 oranges, sliced
16 whole cloves
8 sticks cinnamon
1 to 2 quarts brandy (optional)

Combine the cranberry juice, water, oranges, cloves and cinnamon
sticks in a large saucepan. Simmer for 45 minutes to 2 hours. Discard the cloves and
cinnamon. Pour into a large punch bowl. Stir in the brandy. Float additional
orange slices in the punch for garnish. Serve warm.
Yield: 64 (4-ounce) servings

Nan Graves

Special Occasions
Russian Tea

2 cups orange instant breakfast drink mix
1 cup lemonade instant drink mix
1 1/2 cups sugar
2/3 cup instant tea
1 teaspoon ground cinnamon
1/4 teaspoon ground cloves

Combine the orange drink mix, lemonade drink mix, sugar, tea powder,
cinnamon and cloves in a large bowl and mix well. Store in an airtight container.
Combine 2 tablespoons of the tea mixture with 1 cup hot water for each serving.
Yield: 48 servings

Gail Allen

Shedd Aquarium is the perfect setting for numerous
formal events throughout each year.

Bowle

1 cup crushed or chopped fresh pineapple
1 (10-ounce) package frozen sliced strawberries, thawed
$1/2$ cup sugar
1 cup Cognac
1 bottle Champagne
1 bottle white wine
$1/2$ bottle club soda

Combine the pineapple, strawberries, sugar and Cognac in a large bowl.
Marinate for several hours. Pour over ice in a large punch bowl. Add the
Champagne, wine and club soda, stirring gently.
Yield: 8 servings

Gisela Zech

Caviar Pie

1 small onion, chopped
8 ounces cream cheese, softened
$3/4$ cup sour cream
Romanoff caviar
2 to 3 hard-cooked eggs, chopped
Fresh chives, chopped

Combine the onion, cream cheese and sour cream in a food processor container.
Process until smooth. Spread the mixture over the bottom and up the side of a glass pie
plate. Chill until firm. Spread the caviar evenly over the cream cheese mixture. Top
with the chopped eggs and chives. Serve with baked buttered party rye bread.
Yield: 15 (1-ounce) servings

Betsy Schroeder

Party Cheese Ball

16 ounces cream cheese, softened
2 cups shredded sharp Cheddar cheese
1 tablespoon chopped pimento
1 tablespoon chopped green bell pepper
1 tablespoon finely chopped onion   2 teaspoons Worcestershire sauce
1 teaspoon lemon juice
Dash of cayenne   Dash of salt
Finely chopped pecans

Combine the cream cheese and Cheddar cheese in a bowl, mixing well. Stir in the pimento, green pepper, onion, Worcestershire sauce, lemon juice, cayenne and salt. Shape the mixture into a ball. Chill until firm. Roll in the pecans to coat. Serve with crackers.
Yield: 25 (1-ounce) servings

Louise Kuca

Chicken Coconut Pieces

2 whole boneless chicken breasts
2 eggs, beaten   1 (6-ounce) package flaked coconut
2 to 3 tablespoons butter
1 (8-ounce) jar mango chutney

Rinse chicken and pat dry. Cut into bite-size pieces. Dip in the eggs in a small bowl; roll in the coconut on a plate to coat. Place on a baking sheet. Bake at 375 degrees for 10 to 15 minutes or until the chicken is cooked through and lightly browned. Arrange on a serving plate. Melt the butter in a small saucepan. Stir in the chutney. Serve with the chicken.
Yield: 30 to 40 servings

Mrs. Thomas C. Clark

Pacific Northwest Smoked Salmon Mousse

12 ounces smoked salmon
3 tablespoons lemon juice
2 tablespoons chopped shallots
2 teaspoons chopped dill
3/4 cup melted butter, cooled
1 cup sour cream
Capers and dill sprigs

Flake the salmon into a food processor container, discarding the skin.
Add the lemon juice, shallots, chopped dill and butter. Add the sour cream, reserving
1 tablespoon. Process until smooth. Spoon into a serving bowl. Top with the reserved
dollop of sour cream, capers and dill sprigs. Serve with toasted French bread slices.
May chill for up to 24 hours before serving.
Yield: 12 servings

Ginevra Reed Ralph

Gefilte Fish

This is a Jewish dish usually made before a holiday and for the Sabbath.

1 pound whole whitefish
1 pound whole trout
2 pounds whole pike
4 large onions, cut into fourths
4 carrots, sliced
5 teaspoons salt
1 teaspoon pepper
5 cups water
3 eggs, beaten
Matzo meal

Clean, bone and skin the fish, reserving the heads and bones. Place the reserved heads and bones in a large saucepan with 3 of the onions, 3 of the carrots, 2 teaspoons of the salt, $1/2$ teaspoon of the pepper and 5 cups water. Bring to a boil; reduce heat to medium-low. Simmer 30 to 40 minutes while preparing the fish mixture. Grind the fish finely into a large bowl. Combine the eggs, the remaining onion, carrot, 3 teaspoons salt and $1/2$ teaspoon pepper in a blender container; process until smooth. Stir into the ground fish. Add enough matzo meal to obtain desired consistency. Chill until firm. Shape into 1-inch balls. Strain the stock, discarding the bones, heads and vegetables. Bring to a boil. Drop the fish balls into the stock. Reduce the heat to low. Simmer, covered, for 2 to 3 hours or until the fish balls are puffed. Simmer, uncovered, for 30 minutes longer. Remove the fish balls with a slotted spoon. Strain the stock into a bowl. Chill the fish balls and stock thoroughly. Chop the jelled stock and serve as a garnish with horseradish.

Yield: 20 servings

Margie Eisenberg

Curried Butternut Squash Soup

1 medium butternut squash   1 medium onion, chopped
2 tablespoons butter   1 1/2 teaspoons curry powder
2 medium apples, cored, peeled, chopped   1/2 teaspoon dried thyme
1 quart chicken stock   1/2 to 1 teaspoon salt
1/2 cup whipping cream   White pepper to taste

Peel the squash, discarding the seeds. Cut into 1-inch cubes. Sauté the onion in
the butter in a heavy saucepan until tender but not browned. Add the curry powder.
Cook for 1 minute, stirring frequently. Add the squash, apples, thyme, chicken stock and
salt. Bring to a boil; reduce heat to low. Simmer for 30 to 40 minutes or until the squash is
tender. Pour into a food processor container. Process until puréed. Return to the saucepan.
Add the cream and white pepper. Heat gently until warmed through.
Yield: 4 to 6 servings

Lisa H. Reed

Low-Fat Mushroom Soup

2 cups sliced mushrooms   2 tablespoons minced onion
2 tablespoons butter   1/4 cup flour
1 teaspoon garlic powder   1/4 teaspoon white pepper
1/4 cup dry sherry   1 (10-ounce) can beef consommé
2 cups skim milk   2 teaspoons Worcestershire sauce

Sauté the mushrooms and onion in butter in a heavy saucepan until tender. Add the
flour, garlic powder, white pepper, sherry, consommé, milk and Worcestershire sauce,
stirring well. Simmer over low heat until thickened, stirring frequently. Serve as is, or process
in a blender until puréed. Garnish with croutons or crisp-fried, crumbled bacon.
Yield: 2 servings

Hal Matthies

Special Occasions
Pease's Party Salad

1 head iceberg lettuce
1 head red leaf lettuce
1 head Bibb lettuce
1/2 cup grated Parmesan cheese
6 strips crisp-fried bacon, crumbled
3/4 cup seasoned croutons
1/2 cup vegetable oil
1 1/2 tablespoons white vinegar
Juice of 1/2 lemon
1 egg, beaten
1 teaspoon chopped fresh parsley
2 teaspoons chopped fresh chives
Dash of salt and freshly ground pepper

Tear the iceberg lettuce, red leaf lettuce and Bibb lettuce into a large salad bowl and toss gently to mix. Add the cheese, bacon and croutons. Combine the oil, vinegar, lemon juice, egg, parsley, chives, salt and pepper in a covered container. Shake well to mix. Pour over the lettuce mixture, tossing well to coat. Serve immediately.
Yield: 8 to 10 servings

Robert H. Pease, Jr.

River Point Salad

2 shallots, minced
2 teaspoons Dijon mustard
2 dashes of Worcestershire sauce
1 1/2 tablespoons Tawny Port
2 teaspoons freshly squeezed orange juice
1 teaspoon lemon juice
Salt and pepper to taste
3 tablespoons olive oil
3 Belgian endives
1 large bunch watercress, stems discarded
1/2 cup coarsely chopped walnuts
1 teaspoon soy margarine
1 1/2 pounds medium shrimp, shelled, deveined
1/3 cup crumbled soft goat cheese
1 tablespoon minced fresh orange zest

Combine shallots, Dijon mustard, Worcestershire sauce, port, orange juice, lemon juice, salt and pepper in a small bowl. Add the oil slowly, whisking constantly; set aside. Reserve the 8 outer leaves from the endives. Slice the remaining leaves into matchstick pieces. Chill the endives and watercress in separate covered bowls. Sauté the walnuts in the margarine in a heavy skillet over medium-high heat until browned. Drain on paper towels. Grill the shrimp 6 inches from glowing coals for 1 minute on each side or broil under the broiler. Arrange the reserved endive leaves on 4 salad plates. Toss the chilled endives and watercress separately with the dressing mixture. Arrange over the leaves. Top with the shrimp, walnuts, cheese and orange zest.

Yield: 4 servings

Jorie Butler Kent

Shrimp and Orange Delight

5 large oranges
1 cup whipping cream
$1/2$ cup catsup
2 tablespoons tomato purée
2 tablespoons Scotch whiskey
30 cooked shrimp, peeled, chopped
1 head Boston lettuce, shredded

Cut the tops from the oranges and reserve. Scoop out the pulp and chop; reserve the orange shells. Combine the cream, catsup, tomato purée and whiskey in a mixer bowl. Beat at high speed until thickened. Fold in the chopped orange and the shrimp. Line the reserved orange shells with lettuce. Fill with the shrimp mixture. Replace the reserved orange tops. Serve over crushed ice.
Yield: 5 servings

Laris Gross

Steak Diane

*Al and I have been preparing this recipe for almost twenty years.
It's a fun dish to prepare and great served with long grain and wild rice.*

2 ribeye or filet mignon steaks
Garlic powder to taste
2 1/2 tablespoons butter
2 tablespoons finely minced chives
1 tablespoon finely minced parsley
Salt and pepper to taste
1 tablespoon minced shallots
1 tablespoon Cognac
3 tablespoons sherry

Remove the fat from the steaks and pound flat. Sprinkle with the garlic powder.
Cream 1 1/2 tablespoons of the butter in a bowl with the chives, parsley, salt and pepper;
set aside. Sauté the shallots in the remaining 1 tablespoon butter in a skillet over
medium heat but do not brown. Increase the heat to high. Sear each steak separately
for 30 seconds on each side or to desired degree of doneness. Remove to a warm platter.
Add the Cognac to the skillet and flame, stirring to deglaze the skillet. Reduce the heat.
Add the herbed butter and sherry. Cook until the butter is melted, stirring frequently.
Add the steaks to the skillet. Cook until warmed through, turning once. Place on serving
plates and drizzle with the pan juices. Serve with wild rice and a salad.
Yield: 2 servings

Peggy A. Bock

Dinner-in-a-Pumpkin

An interesting recipe to serve on or near Halloween, each face should be different.

4 (6-inch diameter) pumpkins
1 onion, chopped
2 tablespoons vegetable oil
1 1/2 pounds ground round
2 tablespoons soy sauce
2 tablespoons brown sugar
1 (4-ounce) can sliced mushrooms, drained
1 (10-ounce) can cream of chicken soup
1 1/2 cups cooked rice
1 (8-ounce) can sliced water chestnuts, drained

Paint different faces on each pumpkin with permanent markers or acrylic paint; let dry. Slice off the tops of the pumpkins; clean and discard the seeds. Set aside. Sauté the onion in the oil in a large skillet until tender. Add the ground round. Cook until brown and cooked through, stirring frequently; drain well. Add the soy sauce, brown sugar, mushrooms and soup. Simmer for 10 minutes, stirring occasionally. Stir in the rice and water chestnuts. Spoon the mixture into the pumpkins. Replace the pumpkin tops. Place on a baking sheet. Bake at 350 degrees for 50 minutes or until the pumpkin is tender. Place on individual plates to serve.

Yield: 4 servings

Joan J. Sankovich

Lemon-Glazed Pork Medallions

1 (2 pound) whole pork tenderloin
10 tablespoons flour
2 eggs
2 tablespoons grated Parmesan cheese
$1/2$ cup milk or cream
Salt, pepper, nutmeg to taste
1 cup butter
6 tablespoons lemon juice
Sprigs of parsley

Slice the tenderloin into $1/2$- or $1/4$-inch slices. Pound between sheets of
plastic wrap. Coat the tenderloin slices using 4 tablespoons of the flour. Process the
remaining 6 tablespoons of the flour, eggs, Parmesan cheese, milk, salt, pepper and
nutmeg in a blender container until smooth. Pour the batter into a shallow bowl. Melt
$1/4$ cup of the butter over high heat in a skillet. Dip the medallions into the batter.
Sauté in the butter until cooked through and golden brown on each side, adding more
butter as needed. Remove to a warmed platter. Pour the lemon juice into the skillet,
stirring to deglaze. Cook until the pan drippings are reduced and thickened.
Pour over the medallions. Arrange the parsley on top.
Yield: 4 to 6 servings

Gerd H. Switzer

Fiesta Chicken

*This is a typical dish served in Santa Fe. It is spectacular to
look at as well as a treat to eat.*

4 whole skinless chicken breasts, split
1 1/2 teaspoons salt
1 teaspoon paprika
1/4 cup flour
1/4 cup canola oil
1/4 cup finely chopped onion
1/3 cup catsup
3 tablespoons white wine vinegar
3 tablespoons Worcestershire sauce
1/2 cup white wine
4 cups hot cooked rice
1 (4-ounce) can chopped green chiles, drained
1 large avocado, peeled, sliced

Rinse the chicken and pat dry. Coat with a mixture of the salt, paprika and
flour. Brown the chicken in the oil in a skillet, turning once. Combine the onion, catsup,
vinegar, Worcestershire sauce and wine in a small bowl and mix well. Pour over the
chicken. Simmer, covered, for 45 minutes or until the chicken is tender and cooked through.
Spoon the hot rice in the center of a serving plate. Remove the chicken with a
slotted spoon and arrange around the rice. Stir the green chiles into the pan juices.
Spoon over the chicken. Arrange the avocado slices between the chicken pieces.
Yield: 6 to 8 servings

Diane Horan

Chicken Jubilee

10 to 12 boneless skinless chicken breasts
1 large onion, sliced and separated into rings
3/4 cup chili sauce
1/2 cup white wine
1/2 cup packed brown sugar
1 (16-ounce) can dark sweet pitted cherries
1 (11-ounce) can mandarin oranges

Rinse the chicken and pat dry. Arrange in a 9x13-inch baking dish. Combine the onion rings, chili sauce, wine and brown sugar in a bowl and mix well. Spoon over the chicken. Bake at 400 degrees for 30 minutes, basting occasionally with the pan juices. Pour the undrained cherries and undrained oranges over the chicken. Bake for 15 minutes longer. Serve immediately.

Yield: 10 to 12 servings

Patty Dryer

Low-Fat Gratin of Pheasant

2 whole pheasants
4 (10-ounce) cans low-sodium chicken broth
4 ribs celery   3 to 4 carrots
1 to 2 onions
Freshly ground pepper to taste
Parsley to taste   White wine or water
3 tablespoons margarine
1/4 cup flour
1 cup pheasant or chicken stock
1/2 cup dry white wine   1/2 cup skim milk
1 teaspoon chopped fresh tarragon
1/8 to 1/4 teaspoon cayenne
1 teaspoon Dijon mustard
3 tablespoons grated low-fat Swiss cheese
Salt and pepper to taste
1/4 cup bread crumbs
1 tablespoon margarine

Rinse the pheasants and pat dry. Place in a large stockpot with the chicken broth, celery, carrots, onions, pepper and parsley. Add enough wine or water to cover. Bring to a boil; reduce heat. Simmer until the pheasant is tender. Remove the pheasant and let cool. Chop the pheasant, discarding the skin and bones. Strain the stock, reserving 1 cup; freeze the remaining stock for future use. Melt 3 tablespoons margarine in a large saucepan; add the flour. Cook over low heat for 2 minutes, stirring constantly; remove from heat. Whisk in the reserved pheasant stock and 1/2 cup wine. Simmer until the sauce thickens, whisking constantly. Whisk in the milk, tarragon, cayenne, Dijon mustard, cheese, salt and pepper. Spread a small amount of the sauce over the bottom of a large baking dish. Arrange the pheasant over the sauce. Cover with the remaining sauce. Sprinkle with the bread crumbs and dot with 1 tablespoon margarine. Bake at 375 degrees for 20 minutes or until heated through.

Yield: 4 servings

Mrs. Harry L. Cody

Special Occasions

Wild Game Dinner

1 1/2 cups wild rice
1 orange
1 lemon
1/2 cup port
3/4 cup red currant jelly
1 tablespoon red wine vinegar
Salt and cayenne to taste
1/2 teaspoon prepared mustard
3 whole pheasants, ducks or geese, cleaned and cut up
1/2 to 1 cup milk
1/2 package fish or chicken seasoned coating mix
3 tablespoons olive oil
Freshly chopped thyme to taste

Soak the rice in water in a bowl for 8 to 10 hours; drain. Cook using package directions; keep warm. Peel the orange and lemon, removing white pith. Cut the peels into small strips. Squeeze the orange and lemon and reserve the juices. Place the orange and lemon strips in a small saucepan with a small amount of water. Simmer for 5 minutes. Drain, reserving the juices. Combine the reserved orange and lemon juices and peels with the port, jelly, vinegar, salt, cayenne and mustard in a medium saucepan; mix well. Bring to a boil. Boil for 5 minutes, stirring frequently; reduce heat. Keep warm while preparing the pheasant. Rinse the pheasant and pat dry. Place in a shallow dish and cover with milk. Soak for 20 to 30 minutes, turning occasionally; drain. Dredge in the coating mix. Heat the olive oil in a large skillet. Add the pheasants and the thyme. Fry until brown on all sides and cooked through. Spoon the rice into the center of a serving platter. Arrange the pheasant around the rice. Drizzle with the sauce.

Yield: 4 servings

Thomas C. Clark

Oriental Salmon with Steamed Spinach

1 1/2 pounds salmon fillets
2 tablespoons vegetable oil
3 tablespoons finely chopped scallions
2 tablespoons low-sodium soy sauce
2 cloves of garlic, minced
1 1/2 teaspoons grated gingerroot
Peel and juice of 1 lemon
16 ounces fresh spinach, torn
1 tablespoon sesame seeds, toasted
1 tablespoon chopped scallions

Rinse the salmon and pat dry. Place skin side down in a 9x13-inch dish.
Combine the oil, 3 tablespoons scallions, soy sauce, garlic, gingerroot, lemon peel and
1/2 of the lemon juice in a small bowl and mix well. Pour over the salmon. Marinate,
covered, in the refrigerator for 1 hour. Drain the salmon, reserving the marinade. Grill
over hot coals or place under the broiler for 10 minutes or until the fish flakes easily.
Steam the spinach for 3 to 4 minutes or until slightly wilted. Toss with the remaining lemon
juice and sesame seeds in a bowl. Place an equal amount on 4 plates.
Top with the salmon. Warm the reserved marinade in a saucepan until heated
through. Pour over the salmon. Top with 1 tablespoon scallions.
Yield: 4 servings

Robin Parsons

Oysters Rockefeller à la Bock

This recipe has become a family favorite for Christmas Eve dinner.

2 dozen oysters on the half shell
16 ounces fresh spinach, cooked, drained
1 tablespoon finely chopped shallots
1 clove of garlic, minced
6 scallions, trimmed, chopped
2 ribs of celery, chopped
1/2 cup finely chopped parsley
10 lettuce leaves
1/2 cup melted butter
1 cup bread crumbs
1 tablespoon Worcestershire sauce
Tabasco sauce to taste
3 tablespoons Pernod
3/4 cup grated Parmesan cheese
1/2 cup bread crumbs

Place the oysters and their liquid in a saucepan. Bring to a boil; remove from the heat and set aside. Place the oyster shells on the oven rack. Bake at 450 degrees for 5 minutes; remove and set aside. Combine the spinach, shallots, garlic, scallions, celery, parsley, lettuce and butter in a blender container. Process until puréed, pressing down the mixture with a rubber spatula as needed. Add 1 cup bread crumbs, Worcestershire sauce, Tabasco and Pernod and mix well. Place 1 oyster in each shell. Cover with the spinach mixture. Sprinkle with a mixture of Parmesan cheese and 1/2 cup bread crumbs. Bake at 450 degrees until brown. Serve immediately.

Yield: 4 servings

Peggy A. Bock

Mardi Gras Shrimp Creole

3 onions, chopped
3 to 4 ribs celery, finely chopped
4 cloves of garlic, minced
1 to 2 tablespoons vegetable oil
$1/4$ teaspoon sugar
1 bay leaf
Pinch of thyme
2 (6-ounce) cans tomato paste
2 (16-ounce) cans chopped tomatoes
4 green bell peppers, chopped
$1 1/2$ pounds shrimp, peeled, deveined

Sauté the onions, celery and garlic in the oil in a large deep skillet until browned.
Add the sugar, bay leaf, thyme, tomato paste and tomatoes and mix well. Simmer for
1 to 2 hours, stirring occasionally. Add the green peppers. Simmer for 10 minutes longer.
Add the shrimp. Simmer for 5 minutes longer. Remove and discard the bay leaf. Serve over
rice with a salad and garlic bread. May substitute $1 1/2$ cups frozen chopped onion
and 1 cup frozen chopped green peppers for fresh onion and green peppers.
Yield: 6 to 8 servings

Nan Graves

Torta Pasqualina (Easter Torte)

12 to 14 fresh artichokes
1 1/2 tablespoons lemon juice
1 onion, chopped
2 cloves of garlic, chopped
Oregano to taste
1/4 cup olive oil
1 cup cottage cheese
1/2 cup grated Parmesan cheese
3 eggs, beaten
Pepper to taste
3 sheets phyllo dough
4 eggs
1 egg yolk
1 tablespoon water

Cut off the stems and tough bottom leaves from the artichokes and trim the top leaves. Place stem side up in a saucepan with 1 to 2 inches boiling water and lemon juice. Steam, covered, for 45 minutes or until tender; drain. Remove the leaves and hearts and chop finely; discard the choke. Sauté the onion, garlic and oregano in the olive oil in a large skillet until tender; remove from the heat. Stir in the artichokes, cottage cheese and Parmesan cheese. Add the 3 beaten eggs when the mixture is slightly cooled and mix well. Season with the pepper. Line a deep-dish pie plate or springform pan with the phyllo dough, allowing the sheets to hang over the edge of the dish. Spoon the artichoke mixture into the dish. Make 4 depressions with a large spoon on the surface of the mixture; drop 1 egg into each indentation. Overlap the phyllo dough to cover the top. Brush the phyllo dough with a mixture of the egg yolk and 1 tablespoon water. Bake at 350 degrees for 1 hour. Cool in the pan for several minutes. Remove the torte to a serving dish. May serve hot, at room temperature or cold.

Yield: 6 servings

Laura DeFerrari Front

Corn Pudding

1 medium onion, chopped
1 red bell pepper, chopped (optional)
3 tablespoons butter
1 pound fresh corn, cut from the cob or 1 (16-ounce) package frozen corn, thawed
1 1/4 cups milk or light cream
3 eggs
1/2 cup flour
1/2 teaspoon baking powder
1 cup shredded white Cheddar cheese
Salt and pepper to taste

Sauté the onion and red pepper in the butter in a medium skillet until tender. Add the corn. Cook over low heat for 5 to 10 minutes, stirring frequently. Remove from heat and cool slightly. Beat the milk and eggs in a large bowl. Sift in the flour and baking powder and mix well. Add the corn mixture. Fold in the cheese and season with salt and pepper. Pour into a greased 10x14-inch baking dish. Bake at 375 degrees for 1 hour or until pudding is set and light golden brown.

Yield: 6 to 8 servings

Penelope Mesic

Fruit and Nut Stuffing

*This recipe is from my husband's grandparents who brought
it from Sweden 100 years ago.*

1 loaf white bread, torn into bite-size pieces
20 pitted prunes, chopped
1 apple, chopped
1/4 onion, chopped
2 tablespoons chopped parsley
3/4 cup chopped celery
1/2 teaspoon sage
1 teaspoon salt
Pepper to taste
1 egg, beaten
Toasted sliced almonds or walnuts
1/4 cup melted butter

Combine the bread, prunes, apple, onion, parsley, celery, sage, salt and
pepper in a large bowl, mixing well. Add the egg, almonds and butter, stirring
until moistened. Stuff loosely into a turkey and roast.
Yield: stuffing for an 18-pound turkey

Mrs. Robert Mulvey

Oregon Chanterelle Soufflé

*My daughter and I collect chanterelle mushrooms in coastal mountains
just inland from the rocky shores depicted in the Oceanarium. This recipe allows the full
flavor to come through while stretching the precious commodity of wild mushrooms.*

2 tablespoons butter
2 cups chopped chanterelle mushrooms
3 to 4 shallots, chopped
1 clove garlic, pressed
1/4 cup butter
1/4 cup flour
1 cup milk
2 tablespoons dry sherry
Salt, pepper and cayenne to taste
1/2 cup grated Romano cheese
4 egg yolks, beaten
4 egg whites, stiffly beaten

Melt 2 tablespoons butter in a sauté pan. Add the mushrooms, shallots and garlic.
Cook until all the liquid has evaporated and the mushrooms are dry; set aside. Melt
1/4 cup butter in a saucepan. Stir in the flour; remove from heat. Add the milk slowly, stirring
constantly. Return to low heat. Simmer until slightly thickened, stirring constantly. Add the
sherry, salt, pepper, cayenne and cheese, stirring until the cheese is melted; remove from the
heat. Whisk in the egg yolks. Add the mushroom mixture. Fold in the egg whites. Spoon into
an ungreased 1 1/2-quart soufflé dish. Set the dish into a larger shallow pan of 1 inch hot
water. Bake in the water at 350 degrees for 50 to 60 minutes or until puffed and browned.
Yield: 4 to 6 servings

Ginevra Reed Ralph

Tomato Aspic

1 envelope unflavored gelatin   1 (11-ounce) can tomato juice
1 (12-ounce) can vegetable juice cocktail
1 tablespoon lemon juice   1 teaspoon paprika

Soften the gelatin in half of the tomato juice in a small bowl. Combine the
remaining tomato juice, vegetable juice cocktail and lemon juice in a medium saucepan.
Cook over medium heat until the mixture begins to simmer. Stir in the gelatin mixture and
paprika. Pour into a nonstick 2-quart mold or individual serving bowls. Chill, covered,
until firm. Serve over romaine lettuce. May add 1 cup chopped celery,
1 cup chopped cooked shrimp or 1 chopped avocado.
Yield: 6 servings

Charles C. Haffner, III

Yam Balls

6 to 8 yams   12 large marshmallows
1/4 cup graham cracker crumbs
3 tablespoons melted margarine
3/4 cup packed brown sugar
1/4 cup light corn syrup

Cover the yams in water in a large saucepan and cook until tender; drain and let cool.
Peel the yams. Mash in a large bowl until smooth. Shape the yam mixture around
each marshmallow to form 12 balls. Roll in the graham cracker crumbs. Mix the
margarine, brown sugar and corn syrup in the bottom of a 7x9-inch baking pan.
Arrange the yam balls in the pan. Bake at 350 degrees for 30 minutes.
Yield: 12 servings

Barbara A. Shedd

Special Occasions
Challah

¹/₄ cup honey
¹/₈ cup hot water
1 tablespoon sugar
1 tablespoon (heaping) canola oil
¹/₂ envelope yeast
2 eggs, beaten
4 cups flour
1 cup raisins
1 egg yolk, beaten
Poppy seeds

Combine the honey, hot water, sugar and canola oil in a large bowl. Let stand until lukewarm. Add the yeast, stirring until dissolved. Add the eggs, flour and raisins gradually, beating well after each addition. Knead the dough on a floured surface until smooth and elastic. Cut into three portions and shape into strips. Braid the strips together, pinching the ends to seal. Place on a baking sheet. Brush with the egg yolk. Sprinkle with the poppy seeds. Bake at 400 degrees for 10 minutes. Reduce the oven temperature to 350 degrees. Bake for 45 minutes longer. May substitute sesame seeds for poppy seeds, or use both.

Yield: 1 loaf

Patty Dryer

Spiced Applesauce Bread

1 1/4 cups applesauce
1 cup sugar
1/2 cup vegetable oil
2 eggs, beaten
3 tablespoons milk
2 cups sifted flour
1/2 teaspoon baking powder
1/2 teaspoon cinnamon
1 teaspoon baking soda
1/4 teaspoon salt
1/4 teaspoon nutmeg
1/4 teaspoon allspice
1 cup chopped pecans
1/4 cup packed brown sugar
1/2 teaspoon cinnamon

Combine the applesauce, sugar, oil, eggs and milk in a large bowl and mix well.
Sift the flour, baking powder, 1/2 teaspoon cinnamon, baking soda, salt, nutmeg and
allspice into the applesauce mixture, beating well. Fold in 1/2 cup of the pecans. Shape into
a loaf. Place in a greased 5x9-inch loaf pan. Combine the remaining 1/2 cup pecans,
brown sugar and 1/2 teaspoon cinnamon in a small bowl and mix well. Sprinkle over
the top. Bake at 350 degrees for 1 hour or until the loaf tests done.
Yield: 1 loaf

Nancy H. Hamill

Swedish Pepparnotter Spice Cookies

Any design works with these cookies: make pumpkins at Halloween, turkeys at Thanksgiving, or snowmen and angels at Christmas. For Christmas trees, spread the cookies with honey, dust with confectioners' sugar, and serve the same day; do not store. Plain cookies can be stored in an airtight container for several weeks.

1 cup butter, softened
1 1/2 cups sugar
1 egg, beaten
2 tablespoons honey
1 teaspoon baking soda
1 tablespoon warm water
3 cups flour
2 teaspoons cinnamon
1 teaspoon ginger
1/2 teaspoon ground cloves
1/4 teaspoon allspice

Cream the butter and sugar in a mixer bowl until light and fluffy. Add the egg and honey, beating well. Dissolve the baking soda in warm water in a small bowl. Add to the creamed mixture. Sift the flour, cinnamon, ginger, cloves and allspice together. Add to the creamed mixture, beating well. Dough will be sticky. Shape into an 8-inch round, 2-inch thick circle using floured hands. Wrap in plastic wrap and chill for 4 to 10 hours. Cut into 4 sections. Roll each section out 1/5 inch thick and cut into desired shapes. Place on a nonstick cookie sheet. Bake at 400 degrees for 4 to 7 minutes or until golden brown.

Yield: 40 servings

Geri Pavlick

Swedish Refrigerator Cookies

This is a traditional cookie served during the festival of Santa Lucia on December 13 in Swedish-American communities.

1/2 cup sugar   1 cup butter, softened
2 cups (heaping) flour   Cinnamon   Sugar

Cream 1/2 cup sugar and butter in a mixer bowl until light and fluffy. Add the flour 1 cup at a time, beating well after each addition. Spread a mixture of cinnamon and sugar on a sheet of waxed paper. Shape the dough into a long roll and coat with the cinnamon mixture. Chill for 8 to 10 hours. Cut into slices. Place on a buttered cookie sheet. Bake at 350 to 375 degrees for 10 to 15 minutes or until lightly browned.

Yield: 24 servings

Laura J. Olson

McGrath "Christmas House" Cookies

1 cup salted butter, softened   1/2 cup sugar   Pinch of salt   2 egg yolks
2 1/2 cups flour   1 (18-ounce) jar raspberry preserves
2 cups semisweet chocolate chips   4 egg whites
1 cup sugar   2 cups ground almonds

Cream the butter and 1/2 cup sugar in a mixer bowl until light. Beat in the salt and egg yolks. Add the flour gradually, mixing until dough is very stiff. Spread the dough evenly over a greased 10x15-inch cookie sheet. Bake at 350 degrees for 20 minutes. Spread the preserves over the baked layer; sprinkle with the chocolate chips. Beat the egg whites in a mixer bowl until stiff. Fold in 1 cup sugar and the almonds. Spread evenly over the chocolate chips. Bake for 25 minutes or until lightly browned. Cut into 50 to 60 cookies.

Yield: 50 to 60 servings

Bonnie McGrath

Pumpkin Bars

4 eggs
1²/₃ cups sugar
1 cup corn oil
1 (16-ounce) can pumpkin
2 cups flour
2 teaspoons baking powder
2 teaspoons cinnamon
1 teaspoon baking soda
1 (3-ounce) package cream cheese, softened
¹/₂ cup margarine, softened
1 teaspoon vanilla extract
2 cups confectioners' sugar
Walnut or pecan halves

Beat the eggs, sugar, oil and pumpkin in a mixer bowl until smooth. Add the flour, baking powder, cinnamon and baking soda, mixing well after each addition. Spread the batter in an ungreased 10x15-inch baking pan. Bake at 350 degrees for 25 to 30 minutes. Cool in the pan. Beat the cream cheese, margarine, vanilla and confectioners' sugar in a mixer bowl until light and fluffy. Spread over the cooled baked layer. Top with the walnut or pecan halves. Cut into bars to serve.

Yield: 24 servings

Barbara A. Shedd

Peanut Butter Brittle

2 cups salted Spanish peanuts
2 1/2 cups peanut butter
1/2 teaspoon vanilla extract
1/4 cup water
2 cups sugar
1 1/2 cups light corn syrup
1/2 teaspoon baking soda

Mix the peanuts, peanut butter and vanilla in a bowl; set aside. Combine the
water and sugar in a heavy saucepan. Cook over medium heat until the sugar is
completely dissolved, stirring constantly. Stir in the corn syrup. Cook to 300 to 310 degrees
on a candy thermometer, hard-crack stage; remove from the heat. Stir in the peanut butter
mixture and baking soda. Pour onto 2 greased baking sheets, spreading quickly
with a fork. Let stand until cool. Break into bite-size pieces.
Yield: 3 pounds

Lori Schramm

Poached Pears

6 to 8 firm pears with stems
1 bottle marsala
2 tablespoons sugar
Dash of cinnamon
1 tablespoon cold strong coffee
1 tablespoon rum
1 tablespoon confectioners' sugar
3/4 cup mascarpone cheese

Arrange the pears stem side up in a Dutch oven. Combine the marsala, sugar and cinnamon in a small saucepan. Cook until the liquid begins to simmer. Pour over the pears, adding water if necessary to cover. Bake at 350 degrees for 1 hour or until the pears are tender. Let stand until cool. Drain and reserve the cooking liquid. Pour the reserved liquid into a small saucepan. Bring to a boil. Cook until the liquid is reduced by half. Stir the coffee, rum and confectioners' sugar into the cheese just until mixed and of the consistency of sour cream. Place the pears on individual serving plates. Top with a dollop of the cheese mixture. Drizzle with the reduced liquid.

Yield: 6 to 8 servings

Anne O'Laughlin Scott

Pumpkin Pie with Honey

This recipe was my first attempt at pumpkin pie on our first Thanksgiving together as Mr. and Mrs. It has been a tradition ever since.

2 cups canned pumpkin
$1/2$ teaspoon ground ginger
$1/2$ teaspoon ground cinnamon
1 teaspoon salt
4 eggs, lightly beaten
$1/2$ cup milk
$1/2$ cup whipping cream
1 cup honey
1 unbaked (9-inch) pie shell
1 cup pecan halves
$1/4$ cup butter, softened
1 cup packed brown sugar
$1/2$ cup whipping cream

Combine the pumpkin, ginger, cinnamon and salt in a large mixer bowl, mixing well. Beat the eggs with the milk, $1/2$ cup whipping cream and honey in a medium mixer bowl. Stir into the pumpkin mixture. Pour into the pie shell. Bake at 450 degrees for 10 minutes. Reduce the oven temperature to 375 degrees. Bake for 1 hour longer or until a knife inserted near the center comes out clean. Increase the oven temperature to 400 degrees. Arrange the pecan halves on top of the pie. Mix the butter and brown sugar in a small bowl. Sprinkle over the pie. Bake for 8 to 10 minutes longer or until the butter melts and the pecans are slightly browned. Let stand until cool. Cut into slices. Whip $1/2$ cup whipping cream in a small mixer bowl. Spoon a large dollop over the top of each slice.
Yield: 8 servings

Mrs. Samuel Garre, III

The Clara S. Goehst Fruitcake

*This is an old family recipe that friends and relatives
count on me making every year.*

1 cup butter, softened
1 cup packed brown sugar
1 cup molasses
1¹/₂ ounces brandy
1 cup cold coffee
3 cups flour   4 eggs, beaten
1 teaspoon baking powder
1¹/₂ teaspoons cream of tartar
1 teaspoon ground cloves
1 (1-pound) package dates
16 ounces pecans
3 pounds golden raisins
8 ounces dried figs
2¹/₂ pounds candied mixed fruits, chopped
1 cup flour   Additional brandy

Combine the butter, brown sugar, molasses 1¹/₂ ounces brandy and coffee in a
large mixer bowl. Stir in 3 cups flour gradually, mixing well after each addition. Add the
eggs, baking powder, cream of tartar and cloves, mixing well. Coat the dates,
pecans, raisins, figs and candied fruits with 1 cup flour in a bowl. Stir into the batter. Line six
2-pound loaf pans with waxed paper. Pour batter evenly into the loaf pans. Garnish
with pineapple hearts, cherries halves and pecans. Place a pan of water on the lowest oven
rack. Preheat the oven to 275 degrees. Bake the fruitcakes on the middle oven rack for
1 to 2 hours or until a wooden pick inserted near the center comes out clean. Invert
onto wire racks to cool. Let stand for 24 hours to dry. Soak the sides and bottom of the
cakes in the additional brandy; wrap each fruitcake separately in waxed paper.
Repeat the soaking process 3 times at 1-week intervals. Wrap the fruitcakes tightly with
plastic wrap. May store, tightly wrapped, for up to 1 year.
Yield: 6 fruitcakes

Margaret Goehst Chamales

Old World Fruitcake

My mother-in-law brought this recipe from Europe. It has been a family favorite for almost a century.

1 (16-ounce) package raisins
1 cup water or brandy
1 1/2 cups oil
1 cup sugar
1 teaspoon vanilla extract
5 eggs
1/2 teaspoon ground nutmeg
1 teaspoon ground cinnamon
4 cups flour
2 teaspoons baking soda
2 teaspoons baking powder
Grated peel from 1 lemon
2 cups chopped pecans

Boil the raisins in the water in a small saucepan. Remove from the heat and let stand until cool or soak the raisins in brandy in a bowl for 8 to 10 hours. Drain and set aside, reserving the liquid. Cream the oil, sugar and vanilla in a mixer bowl until light and fluffy. Add the eggs 1 at a time, beating well after each addition. Stir in the reserved liquid. Sift the nutmeg, cinnamon, flour, baking soda and baking powder together. Add to the batter gradually, mixing well. Fold in the lemon peel, pecans and raisins. Pour into a greased and floured 9x13-inch cake pan. Bake at 350 degrees for 1 hour or until the cake tests done.

Yield: 15 servings

Lisbet O. Temple

Special Occasions
Poppy Seed Cake

¹/3 cup poppy seeds
1 cup yogurt
1 cup butter, softened
1¹/2 cups sugar
4 eggs
1 teaspoon vanilla extract
2¹/2 cups flour
2 teaspoons baking powder
1 teaspoon baking soda
¹/2 teaspoon salt
¹/3 cup sugar
1 teaspoon cinnamon

Stir the poppy seeds into the yogurt in a small bowl. Chill for 8 to 10 hours. Cream the butter and 1 1/2 cups sugar in a mixer bowl until light and fluffy. Add the eggs 1 at a time, beating well after each addition. Stir the vanilla into the yogurt mixture. Sift the flour, baking powder, baking soda and salt together. Add to the creamed mixture alternately with the yogurt mixture, beginning and ending with the flour mixture and beating well after each addition. Pour half of the batter into a greased bundt pan. Top with a mixture of 1/3 cup sugar and cinnamon. Cover with the remaining batter. Bake at 350 degrees for 1 hour. Cool in the pan. Garnish with a dusting of confectioners' sugar.

Yield: 16 servings

Mary Jane Drews

Index